W9-CFJ-457

Bargain Shopping
in Palm Beach & Broward Counties

200+ Consignment, Thrift and Vintage Shops in Palm Beach, Boca Raton, Fort Lauderdale, and more

Women's, Children's & Men's Clothes & Accessories,
Jewelry, Designer Handbags, Shoes, Vintage,
Home Décor, Furniture, Gifts, Estates,
Affordable Antiques, Art & Collectibles & More

by
Paulette Cooper Noble

The Happy Shopper

FOR MORE COPIES OF THIS BOOK, GO TO
WWW.SHOPPINGINFLORIDA.NET

FOR CHANGES AND UPDATES,
SEE FACEBOOK: SHOPPINGINFLORIDA
To reach the author e-mail shopinpalmbeach@aol.com
Follow us on FACEBOOK: SHOPPINGINFLORIDA

Published by:

PoloPublishing of Palm Beach
Post Office Box 621
Palm Beach, FL 33480
www.shoppinginflorida.net
FACEBOOK: SHOPPINGINFLORIDA

ISBN: 978-0-9914013-2-1

Photographs by Paulette Cooper Noble

Polo photo by Lenny Hirschfield
Back cover photo by Tina Valant
Back cover copy by Ann Schwartz
Cover design by Mandy McLaughlin

E-mail *shopinpalmbeach@aol.com* to reach the author.
Made in the United States of America.
Published by:
POLOPUBLISHING OF PALM BEACH
Post Office Box 621 | Palm Beach, FL 33480
www.shoppinginflorida.net

Table of Contents

INTRODUCTION: Acknowledgments, Notice & Author's Note.....**4 & 5**

PART 1: PALM BEACH COUNTY
Boca Raton...**7**
Special: How to Tell if a Designer Handbag is Real.................**18**
Special: The Most Upscale Consignment & Vintage Shops.......**13**
Delray Beach..**25**
Jupiter & Juno Beach..**39**
Lake Worth – Lake Avenue......................................**46**
Lake Worth (Other)..**52**
Lantana & Boynton Beach..**58**
North Palm Beach & Lake Park.................................**63**
Northwood..**66**
Palm Beach..**70**
Palm Beach Gardens...**85**
Tequesta...**92**
West Palm Beach – South Dixie Highway....................**95**
West Palm Beach, Wellington & More.......................**105**

PART 2: BROWARD COUNTY
Broward – West of Fort Lauderdale.............................**113**
(Coral Springs, Plantation & Sunrise)
Broward – South of Fort Lauderdale...........................**119**
(Cooper City, Davie, Hollywood, Pembroke Pines)
Deerfield Beach..**123**
Fort Lauderdale...**127**
Oakland Park & Wilton Manors.................................**132**
Pompano Beach..**138**

MORE STORES **143**
MORE: About the Author, Researcher & Editor.............**146**
Interview with Paulette Cooper Noble, The Happy Shopper.....**147**

Acknowledgments

This book is dedicated to my father, TED COOPER, who lived to almost 100 without ever being inside a consignment, thrift or vintage shop... Thanks especially to LISA PETERFREUND for her hard work, ideas, and support, which made this book possible, and to the great contributions of SUSAN COLEMAN, who worked on the first edition of my shopping book.... And most of all, to my wonderful husband, PAUL NOBLE, for patiently waiting while I worked 16 hours a day to write this book, and for (rightly) believing that I was out working when I was out shopping.

Important Notices

1) In today's economy, stores are going out of business. Happily, though, new ones are sprouting up. Please call the shops in this book before you go to make certain nothing has changed, including the hours listed here. They are all in season and not summer hours, which may differ. And double-check the Facebook page (SHOPPINGINFLORIDA) to make sure they're still in business.
2) This is a book for shoppers, not consignors. No recommendations are made about consigning anything at any place in this book. The author has heard too many complaints from people who have consigned clothes, antiques, furniture, etc. She therefore takes absolutely no responsibility for what happens if anyone does consign something anyplace that they read about here.
3) If you come upon any errors or changes from what you read here, or you wish to make suggestions, please feel free to e-mail me at shoppinginflorida@gmail.com.
4) Additional copies can be purchased at www.shoppinginflorida.net.
5) For updates, plus new shops, and changes for places already in this book, visit my Facebook page: SHOPPINGINFLORIDA
6) All shops say whether they're consignment or thrift; thrift shops are usually less expensive but the clothes in them are generally not of the same quality as consignment, unless they're a "quality thrift."

Paulette Cooper Noble
The Happy Shopper

Author's Note

Some shoppers get pleasure when they spend money; others when they save it. If you belong to that second group, this book is for you.

Even before Cheap Chic became fashionable, many of you – sometimes secretly – had already discovered the joy of bagging a designer handbag at a consignment shop, of encountering a treasure in a thrift shop, of rediscovering a favorite gown at a vintage shop, or of finding a barely-used piece of furniture in a consignment store that fits perfectly into that lonely corner of your home. If this is you, this is a book for you.

Some bargain hunters like high-end consignments, others rock-bottom thrifts. Some seek Salvation Army, others salvation in Armani.

There's something for everyone in this book. There are expensive women's and men's consignment shops, and there are thrift shops where you can bag a bargain for a buck.

This book is divided into geographical regions (Palm Beach & Broward Counties) and then alphabetically within the county. (See Table of Contents on p. 3)

Almost every one of the 200 stores was personally checked out by me at least once. I know what you're thinking. "Wow – she calls going to stores work?" But it was hard work. And now I'm glad to be finished with it, and I can do something for fun – like shopping.

In fact, in some ways this book is like shopping: serendipitous. There is no index of stores in the back. I want people to skim through the sections, and discover places they didn't know existed – and get in their cars and go to them. That's what makes shopping – and hopefully reading this book – fun.

But don't overspend in this economy. Just remember The Happy Shopper's motto: You don't have to spend a hundred to look like a million.

Paulette Cooper Noble
The Happy Shopper

PART 1:
PALM BEACH COUNTY

Including

Boca Raton 7

Delray Beach 25

Jupiter & Juno Beach.................................... 39

Lake Worth - Lake Avenue 46

Lake Worth (Other) 52

Lantana & Boynton Beach 58

North Palm Beach & Lake Park 63

Northwood 66

Palm Beach.. 70

Palm Beach Gardens.................................... 85

Tequesta 92

West Palm Beach - South Dixie Highway.... 95

West Palm Beach, Wellington & Other 105

Boca Raton

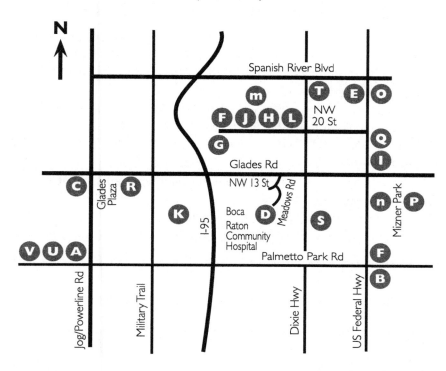

A..... Cocoblue (p. 8)

B..... Coconut Consignment Company (p. 9)

C..... Consignment Exchange (p. 9)

D..... Debbie-Rand Memorial Thrift (p. 10)

E..... Dzines (p. 11)

F..... Encore Plus (p. 12)

G..... Family Safe Haven (p. 12)

H.... Florence Fuller Thrift Shop (p. 14)

I........ Goodwill Boca Boutique (p. 15)

J........ Hospice By The Sea Chest Thrift Shop (p. 15)

K..... Legacy (p. 16)

L...... Levis JCC Thrift Shop (p. 16)

M.... Papillion Vintage Home (p. 17)

N.... Past Perfect (p. 19)

O.... Perfectly Imperfect (p. 19)

P...... Razzamatazz of Boca Raton (p. 20)

Q.... ReView (p. 20)

R..... Serendipity (p. 21)

S...... Show & Tell Consignments (p. 22)

T..... Tri County Humane Society Thrift Shop (p. 23)

U.... Will & Emma's Closet (p. 23)

V..... Zanna Jane's West Boca (p. 24)

7

SPECIAL SHOPPING TOUR –
HIGH-END CONSIGNMENT SHOPS IN BOCA RATON

Within a small area near Mizner Park are two high-end women's consignment shops. Coming off of A1A, start at **ENCORE PLUS**, a high-end women's consignment shop is at 281 E. Palmetto Park Road. (See p. 12.)

Continue west and you're soon on Federal. If you go north, and then right a few blocks up on SE 2nd, there's a little mall where you'll find **RAZZAMATAZZ OF BOCA RATON**, a pricey women's consignment shop next to Mizner Park at 116 NE 2nd St. (See p. 20.)

NOTE: If you're looking for home décor and gifts, **COCONUT CONSIGNMENT** at 68 S. Federal Hwy., is great. (See p. 9.)

FOR ANOTHER SHOPPING TOUR OF BOCA, SEE P. 14.

SEE BELOW FOR MORE SHOPS IN BOCA RATON.

WOMEN'S CLOTHING & ACCESSORIES (CONSIGNMENT)

COCOBLUE

www.cocoblueboutique.com
Del Mar Village Plaza 7042 Beracasa Way
Boca Raton 33433 / (561) 367-7177
OPEN: Tues.-Sat. 11-4

This smallish but stylish store has a very boutique-y feel about it, and even if it's slightly out of the way for you, it's worth the visit.
They sell fabulous designer clothing, handbags and shoes – in every shape, color and size – plus jewelry and clothing of local designers. You'll definitely find something to spice up your wardrobe. This cozy consignment shop has won a number of awards, and rightly so, for their mid-range and higher-end women's, handbags, and shoes. They pack a lot in, without it seeming crowded. And the inventory is constantly changing.
DON'T MISS: There's a 50% off section in the back.

FURNITURE & HOME DÉCOR (CONSIGNMENT)

COCONUT CONSIGNMENT COMPANY

68 S. Federal Hwy. / Boca Raton 33432
(561) 362-7040
OPEN: Mon.-Sat. 10:30-5

I've been a great fan of this shop for decades, because it's a terrific furniture, home décor and gift shop that's easy to get to since it's one block south of Palmetto Park Road on Federal Highway. It's a bit hard to get around in the shop, though, because it's so full. But that's fine, because it gives you lots of great things to explore, and plenty of good things to buy.

Furniture hunters can easily bag their game, OK, their couch, chair, or whatever they're looking for here. Coconut Consignment's motto is "unusual things from unusual places," and they could have added "at unusual prices" – unusually low for this type of fine merchandise.

Accessories and gifts are in practically pristine condition, and everywhere you turn, or look, something unique and attractive pops up that you'll want to buy to upgrade or improve your place.

DON'T MISS: There's a small section to the right in the back with fun knickknacks.

SALES INFORMATION: They often offer everything for 10% off.

WOMEN'S CLOTHING & ACCESSORIES (CONSIGNMENT)

CONSIGNMENT EXCHANGE

https://www.facebook.com/consignmentexchange
Shoppes at Boca Grove 21073 Powerline Rd., Suite 23 / Boca Raton 33433
(561) 852-7644
OPEN: Mon. 11-4; Tues.-Fri. 10-6; Sat. 10-5

There's a reason I have been coming to this two-room heavily-stocked shop for almost two decades. Even before I moved to Florida, when I would come here to visit relatives, I would immediately run to this shop. That's because I'm just one of many fans of a place with well-priced, gently-worn apparel and lots of handbags, glasses, and jewelry for women of all ages. That also includes younger ones, which is a plus, since most women's consignment shops ignore this age group.

But young people will find as much to please them as will their older counterparts, including a large collection of designer blue jeans. Still, you don't have to be young or old to delight in all the terrific clothes and accessories. The latter are their forte, and the stunning jewelry, designer and vintage, with prices from $14 for hoops to $600 for Chanel. Don't miss the glass showcase immediately to your left when you enter, or those sometimes hidden in the back of the front room.

There's an impressive amount of beautiful handbags throughout (including some hard-to-find vintage ones) with all the big designer names as well as more affordable bags around. Their collection of designer shoes and designer glasses is also extensive, and not that expensive.

Boutique clothes are mixed in, mostly in the front section. The room in the back has even more clothes, handbags and shoes, and plenty to choose from in their 50% off rack. This was always one of the great women's clothing consignment shops in Boca, and now it's twice as good, no three times as good, since they added a third room to their already two well-stocked rooms. Also, visit their Facebook page to find out about their special sales – even though the prices are already fabulous. (And the merchandise top-notch.)

CLOTHES & MISCELLANEOUS (THRIFT)

DEBBIE RAND MEMORIAL THRIFT SHOPPE
903 Meadows Rd. / Boca Raton 33486 / (561) 395-2208
OPEN: Mon.-Sat. 9-4; Sun 12-4

"We've sold everything except airplanes, and that includes cars and even a cemetery plot," said a salesperson here. But the best things they sell at this large hard-to-find thrift shop are the women's clothes and accessories in their boutique.

You may be rewarded with some excellent labels, although generally not in typical tip-top consignment-shop condition. Still, you won't pay those kinds of prices either for a Judith Leiber or Fendi bag, both of which have been bagged by savvy shoppers in this secret area. Still, don't expect too much. I found one Vuitton bag in such condition I would never wear it, and I was told that the volunteer workers sometimes grab the good stuff. But that's true in all these places, so you just have to be lucky.

WOMEN'S CLOTHING & ACCESSORIES (CONSIGNMENT)

DZINES *Beads*

www.dzinesconsignment.com
Facebook: dzines consignment
3333 N. Federal Hwy. / Boca Raton 33431
(561) 362-0234
OPEN: Mon. 11-3; Tues.-Sat; 10:30-5:30

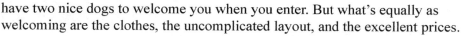

There are new owners in an old consignment spot and it's worth coming to visit them and their shop. Paula and her daughter Melissa have two nice dogs to welcome you when you enter. But what's equally as welcoming are the clothes, the uncomplicated layout, and the excellent prices.

They sell lovely women's consigned clothes and accessories nicely and neatly displayed. Also, there are lots of great sale items. For example, in the back may be half-price racks and a "clearance corner" offering even bigger discounts. Like the Christian Dior robe here for $3! While another Christian Dior not on sale was $15. So you know you'll do well here. I always stop by when I'm going down to Boca, and have never been disappointed.

HOME ACCENT SHOP NEARBY: PERFECTLY IMPERFECT CONSIGNMENTS right next door carries home décor, custom art, and gifts.

If men can run the world, why can't they stop
wearing neckties? How intelligent is it to start
the day by tying a little noose around your neck?

– Linda Ellerbee

BARGAIN SAVING TIP: Usually thrift shops that serve a cause have better merchandise. For example, thrifts that support charities for pets or a disease (say, diabetes), get donations from people who support that charity. The donors may be willing to give good things away to a thrift (rather than trying to get money from a consignment shop for it), knowing that the money their merchandise brings in will help their favorite cause. (I give everything to pet charities.)

Women's Clothing & Accessories (Consignment)

ENCORE PLUS

www.encoreplusinc.com
TWITTER PAGE: @EncorePlusInc
281 E. Palmetto Park Rd. / Boca Raton 33432
(561) 391-3812
OPEN: Mon.-Fri. 10-6; Sat. 10-5

Encore Plus used to be in Deerfield but they have moved to the Boca consignment area. Hallelujah! This was always a beautiful shop with very very upscale merchandise, but now they have a back section with sale items for the more budget-conscious high-end shopper.

Happily, the new shop is about three times larger than the old one, and clothes are spread out nicely so you feel that you're in a boutique and not a resale shop. They still have the same beautiful clothes and accessories (and two stunning and friendly owners!) Plus, their shoes are practically wearable art, making them a shoe-in for best high-end footwear.

This "designer resale boutique" is definitely one of the most upscale consignment shops in Southeast Florida. Their clothes come from some of the most sought-after designers in the world, and if you don't mind paying a little more for the quality, then Encore Plus is a place you won't want to miss. Most of the clothes and accessories here have supposedly been worn but you'd surely never know it.

Women's, Men's & Children's Clothes & Home Goods (Thrift)

FAMILY SAFE HAVEN THRIFT STORE & BOUTIQUE

familysafehaven.org
146 NW 20th St. / Boca Raton 33431 / (561) 368-3339
OPEN: Mon.-Fri. 10:30 -5:30; Sat. 10-6.

This is a hard to describe place because some of it is pretty awful, but there are a few good things that could make it worthwhile to visit IF you happen to be at the three better thrift shops at Plum Park across the street. (See JC p. 16, Hospice p. 15, Fuller p. 14) This one is situated in the strip mall across from Plum Park.

Sometimes there's a lone (or maybe two) better garments for women, and they're usually right up front so that makes them easy to spot. You can skip most of the rest of the clothes, especially the children's in the back. But the men's clothes to the right as you enter sometimes features something good, and occasionally so does the back of the checkout counter, although the costume jewelry in front of it is a joke. And you can certainly skip the used underwear in bins (ugh) near the counter.

In back of the counter and around it, you'll sometimes find some good small appliances and computer-related products. A recent check of the place turned up a great scanner at an excellent price – but everything was in Spanish. Even if you speak a smattering of the language, could you really set up a complicated piece of equipment using what may be your second language?

The second room to the left again leaves much to be desired in the clothing although there are lots of (used-looking) shoes. Bottom line: plenty of stuff there (stuff being a good way to describe it) but not plenty of good stuff. . But in back toward the right are kitchen, household items, and appliances. You might even find something at a good price. Hopefully in English.

THE 16 MOST UPSCALE (EXPENSIVE) WOMEN'S CLOTHING CONSIGNMENT & VINTAGE SHOPS IN PALM BEACH & BROWARD COUNTIES

ATTITUDES (Palm Beach, P. 72) • AVENUE REVUE (Palm Beach, P. 72) • BALATRO VINTAGE (Palm Beach, P. 73) • CLASSIC COLLECTIONS (Palm Beach, P. 76) • COUTURE UPSCALE (Fort Lauderdale - Oakland Park, P. 132) • DEJA VU (Palm Beach, P. 77) • DINA C'S FAB & FUNKY (West Palm Beach, P. 101) • ENCORE PLUS (Boca Raton, P. 12) • FASHIONISTA (Palm Beach, P. 79) • JENNIFER'S DESIGNER EXCHANGE (Palm Beach Gardens, P. 87) • MAXIMS OF PALM BEACH (Palm Beach, P. 81) • PALM BEACH VINTAGE (West Palm Beach-Dixie, P. 104) • RAZAMATAZ (Palm Beach, P. 83) • RAZZAMATAZZ OF BOCA RATON (Boca Raton, P. 20) • SERENDIPITY (Boca Raton, P. 21) • WORTH REPEATING (Fort Lauderdale-Wilton Manors, P. 138)

FLORENCE FULLER THRIFT SHOP

Plum Park / 141 NW 20th St. / Boca Raton 33486 / (561) 391-9379
OPEN: Mon.–Sat. 10-5; Sun. 12-4

This is the first of the thrift shops to the left when you enter Plum Park, thrifter's heaven. It's been in existence close to 30 years, and it's large and full of a variety of merchandise. It's easy to shop here because it's so well organized. Particularly good is the children's department to the left when you enter, as well as the furniture around the rest of the room. Indeed, they've had some amazing rugs and couches.

SPECIAL SHOPPING TOUR – THRIFT SHOPS IN BOCA RATON

A trip to the three thrifts of Boca in Plum Park at 141 NW 20th Street – all with great boutique sections– plus a visit to three other resale shops nearby make for a great shopping day. But watch carefully as you approach Plum Park because it comes up quickly right past Dixie Highway on the north side of 20th Street, and has a small easy-to-miss entrance. Start up front at:

FLORENCE FULLER THRIFT SHOP #C4 (See p. 14.)

LEVIS JCC THRIFT SHOP #C9 (See p. 16.)

Then go to the back of the mall and visit:

HOSPICE BY THE SEA #E2 – (See p. 15.)

Ready for more? At the back of the mall is a great new home décor with refinished and refurbished furniture called **PAPILLON VINTAGE HOME** (See p. 17.)

Also, outside of Plum Plaza but in the area is **ReView**, a woman's consignment shop in the "Fifth Avenue Shopping Center," also called the "Publix Mall" at 1946 NE 5th Ave, 1 block south of 20th Street. (See p. 20.)

FOR AN UPSCALE CONSIGNMENT TOUR OF BOCA SEE P. 8.

SEE THIS CHAPTER FOR MORE BOCA RATON SHOPS.

GOODWILL: BOCA BOUTIQUE

www.gulfstreamgoodwill.org
1662 N. Federal Hwy. / Boca Raton 33432 / (561) 362-8662
OPEN: Mon.-Sat. 9-7; Sun. 10-6

I have watched this once great thrift shop deteriorate, until it's hardly worth going there anymore. The housewares/gifts along with the shoe section are what's best here, but the boutique and "better" items have become increasingly disappointing. One great buy here is furniture, but there's almost no room for much with all the clothes and knickknacks. Yet the small selection they offered – probably donated from beautiful homes in the area – was excellent, and so were the prices. But the shoes. Ah. If you're there, or nearby, run, do not walk (at least until you've bought some of their shoes) to their shoe section. Most aren't very new but every once in a while.... bingo.

HOSPICE BY THE SEA CHEST THRIFT SHOP

Plum Park / 141 NW 20th St. / Boca Raton 33486 / (561) 338-4030
OPEN: Tue.-Sat. 10-4:30

This is now the lone thrift store in the back of Plum Plaza (JCC and Florence Fuller are in the front) and it used to be close to a dump. But wow have they changed!

They've joined forces with the Hospice of Palm Beach County, which runs that terrific thrift shop in Juno Beach (see p. 41.) The result is when you come here now, you'll now find some very good furniture and home décor. Unfortunately, a lot of it costs more than it did before, and it's harder to bargain like it used to be, because if you try, they'll tell you they can't do it because they're no longer in charge. Whatever.

Even so, what wonderful bargains are here to be had, in other words, good merchandise at thrift store prices.

A large almost new white couch was only $259, and in an-easy-to miss section on the left hand side when you walk in, on the back wall, were some really interesting pieces for a fraction of their worth. There's a large book and knickknack area to the right, where the Happy Shopper picked up a small Limoges plate for $5.

The boutique in back still carries some better items, with some good women's boutique and men's as well. Indeed, some of the men's merchandise is the best outside of a consignment shop at much less money. The crummy clothes that were once to the left where the furniture now is has moved to the back as well, on the right. But you may find something so look all around. It's almost as good as JCC (see p. 16) in the same mall. (Well, not quite.)

FURNITURE, HOME DÉCOR, & ESTATES (CONSIGNMENT)

LEGACY   *2980 N Federal*
https://www.facebook.com/LegacyEstateLiquidationSales
~~1200 Clint Moore Rd. Suite 11~~ / Boca Raton 33487 / (561) 922-3794
OPEN: Fri. Sat. (Sun. in season only) from 10-3

The showroom for the large estate and liquidation sale company carries everything from quality furniture to designer bags, costume jewelry, garage sale items, kitchenware and a fantastic selection of goods. Nancy Rosenthal also owns a great children's consignment shops, WILL & EMMA'S CLOSET. Legacy's showroom is only open a limited amount of time, probably because she's out buying the rest of the time. What a life!

CLOTHES, FURNITURE & MISCELLANEOUS (THRIFT)

LEVIS JCC THRIFT SHOP
Plum Park / 141 NW 20th St. / Boca Raton 33431 / (561) 368-3665
OPEN: Mon.-Sat. 10-5; Sun. 11-4

This is the second of the fabulous thrift shops when you enter Plum Park, and they probably have the best merchandise of the quartet. Their prices are sometimes a bit higher, but the merchandise is often, frankly, better.

Incredible bargains are all around you. One shopper joyfully reported that during one of their many sales, she purchased her son-in-law a Christian Dior jacket, a Brooks Brother shirt and Armani pants – all for $35. You'll also find some merchandise that is not routinely carried by the other three large thrifts in this mall. They feature more Judaica, generally in one of the glass showcases by the entrance. Plus vintage clothes, some known designers, and at prices closer to a thrift shop than a usually quite expensive vintage store.

SALES INFORMATION: Everything in the store is usually 50% and sometimes they have additional sales over that.

HOME DÉCOR (CONSIGNMENT) & REFINISHED, REFURBISHED SMALL FURNITURE

PAPILLON VINTAGE HOME

www.papillonvintagehome.com, &
www.facebook.com/papillonvintagehome.com
& www.etsy.com/shop/papillonvintagehome
141 NW 20th St. / Boca Raton 33431
(954) 803-4942
OPEN: Tues.-Sat. 10:30-4

It's a relief after going through the dark and cavernous thrifts in this mall to come into a bright, clean-looking new shop with a cheerful owner who's happy to wait on you. (Most of the sales people in the thrifts seem too busy to bother.) There's a lot of beautiful hand-painted furniture here – much of it has a nice continental flair – and it turns out the artistic genius is the owner, Laura Hinkes. She'll be also be happy to teach you how to paint, stencil and refinish furniture. But it'll probably not come out as well, so you might as well choose to have her do it for you.

"The reason I moved into this mall was so people could buy some thrift furniture, and bring it here to be refinished," she explained. Laura also has a room where she teaches classes in painting and refinishing furniture.

Besides her own pieces, there are a lot of lovely pillows, chairs, small chests and drawers, and even jewelry. She calls "upscale elegance" these one-of-a-kind, hand-finished vintage furniture, antiques and architectural salvage pieces. Whatever you call it, Papillon is a wonderful addition to this mall. In fact, it would be wonderful anywhere.

SHOP NEARBY: DAWNS DESIGNER DUDS AND DECORZ (561) 655-1991. This eclectic emporium is right next to Papillon so it would be silly not to stop by. If it's open, since the hours seem variable. So is the merchandise, which includes a small amount of clothes, jewelry, bags, jeans, and knickknacks.

*"I hold my wife's hand wherever we go.
If I let go she goes shopping."*
– Rodney Dangerfield

10 WAYS TO TELL IF A DESIGNER HANDBAG (CHANEL, VUITTON, BURBERRY, ETC.,) IS REAL

Gone are the days when people used to sell bags stamped "Goochi," or buy fake Rolexes whose second hands moved spastically instead of smoothly so everyone knew it wasn't real. Now, it's often impossible to tell if a product is counterfeit, especially when it's an expensive knock-off.

Actually, in some ways, a fake may look better, since many real bags are made by hand, and fakes by machines. But here are some tip-offs that may help you tell if an expensive "designer" handbag is real.

1) See if the pattern aligns correctly. For example, look at the Burberry bag from the side; the stripes on the seams (where the bag opens) should look like a continuation of the pattern on both sides. And the red line is always in the middle. Similarly, in a quilted Chanel, the triangle should continue below the flap. In other words, if the top part of the triangle pattern is on the flap, when you close the bag, the bottom of the triangle should smoothly blend in so it's a real triangle.

2) Check the lining, which is where counterfeiters often scrimp to save money. Not only should it not look cheap, but it shouldn't pull away from the sides.

3) Look at the embossing or monogramming of the name, which should be very clean, clear and straight. Take Burberry, for example. The knight should be defined and look like a knight with a lance on a horse. Fakes have horses that may look fat and slightly out of shape. The alligators on a real Lacoste will have stitching that clearly show the animal's teeth.

4) Check the hardware. Make sure the zipper moves smoothly and doesn't catch, and that it doesn't feel light and cheap – and like plastic. And make sure the hardware is all the same color and finish.

5) Watch out for incomplete logos. A dead giveaway that a Vuitton is fake, for example, is if the LV is cut. The "Wall Street Journal" pointed out that a Louis Vuitton doesn't cut away part of their logo, say, when the letters reach the seam. Nor would they be interrupted by a zipper.

6) Patterns should mirror themselves. For example, on a Vuitton, if one end has two stars and two circles and an LV, you'll have the same configuration on the other side of the handbag.

7) If the bag comes with a booklet or card, it should not be photocopied.

8) Smell it. An article in foxbusiness.com pointed out that leather should smell like leather – not glue, rubber or chemicals.

9) Trust your instinct. If I wonder if it's real it probably isn't; when it's real I look at it and know. Tami Rowe of City Girl has another method: "If my heart starts fluttering, then it's a real Chanel."

10) Finally, if it's too inexpensive, it probably isn't real.

18

FURNITURE, JEWELRY & HOME DÉCOR (CONSIGNMENT)

PAST PERFECT

99 NE Mizner Blvd. / Boca Raton 33432
(561) 338-5656
OPEN: Mon.-Sat. 9:30-5:30; Sun. 12-5

This large five-room shop one block south of Mizner Park has been around for 32 years, and has some nice furniture, art, and decorative home accessories. They also sell some especially good costume jewelry, which may be reduced if it's been here for over a month.

NOTE: Past Perfect has a CLEARANCE CENTER at 1801 NW 1st. Ave., off Glades Road. Call (561) 544-0950 for more information.

Open Tues.-Sat., 10-5.

CONSIGNMENT SHOP NEARBY: RAZZAMATAZZ OF BOCA RATON. (See p. 20.)

HOME DÉCOR & GIFTS

PERFECTLY IMPERFECT

perfectlyimperfectconsignment.com
3333 N. Federal Hwy. #2B / Boca Raton 33431
(561) 756-9267
OPEN: Mon.-Sat. 10:30-5

The Happy Shopper has made many happy visits here because it's right next to a great clothing consignment store: DZines (See p. 11) Perfectly Imperfect's home décor and gifts are more perfect than imperfect, and they carry unusual and unique consigned items in pristine condition. Says the owner, Jennifer Gaffey, "We display them in a way people can envision the items in their own home."

The prices are really really good, and if you need a gift item, everything looks so new here that no one will know you paid anything less than retail for it (which of course you should never do anyway).

In addition to coffee table books, totes, a bit of estate jewelry, art, lighting and more, you'll occasionally find something pet-related. That's because owner Jennifer loves dogs, especially her tiny Madigan, the four-legged "Head of Security and Official Greeter" who may greet you when you come in.

WOMEN'S CLOTHING & ACCESSORIES (CONSIGNMENT)

RAZZAMATAZZ OF BOCA RATON

116 NE 2nd St. / Boca Raton 33432
(561) 394-4592
OPEN: Mon.-Sat. 10-5

 This small but beautiful very high-end consignment boutique has truly spectacular merchandise. Just about everything there is top-designer gently-worn clothes and accessories that look brand new. They don't have a lot of merchandise, but it's mostly quality clothes that will last for a long time. They also have a large selection of designer jeans.

 Two glass cabinets at the entrance will wow you with the high-end designer handbags. While they often have sale merchandise to the right toward the back, prepare to pay big bucks for most of what's here.

WOMEN'S CLOTHING & ACCESSORIES (CONSIGNMENT)

ReVIEW

www.reviewclothinginc.com
Facebook: reView Clothing
1946 NE 5th Ave. / Boca Raton 33431
(561) 544-0111
OPEN: Tues..-Sat. 11-4:30

 When lots of people told me to visit this place, I knew I had to go. Now that I've gone, I can recommend the clothes and accessories - and the owner who's friendly, helpful and moved here from Colorado 1 1/2 years ago.

 She's situated in a large mall (the 5th Avenue Shopping Center anchored by Publix) and has stocked only attractive clothes at excellent prices along with a large selection of jewelry. Some of it wonderfully bling with a bit of Colorado thrown in. Although she has many designer names throughout - and provides her increasingly loyal customer base with the opportunity to sign up on her wish list for the high-end designer names - she also has unique merchandise you'll want to touch and feel. "I don't carry Chico's and Banana Republic kind of clothes," she explained, adding that what she chooses to sell "is hip, a bit of edge, and lots of trends–including designer jeans at wonderful prices." It obviously works because she's been in this spot a year and has more than 200 consignors. About 10% of the accessories is purchased directly through manufacturers. She sells these to dress up all the wonderful clothing that arrives from her clients.

THRIFT SHOP NEARBY: ANIMAL AID INC., at 2266 N. Dixie Hwy. Unless you're a dedicated thrifter who never misses a shop, you can miss this one. But if you're an animal lover (and aren't we all?) the main reason to go there is to buy something that will aid distressed animals.

WOMEN'S CLOTHING & ACCESSORIES (CONSIGNMENT)

SERENDIPITY

www.consignmentboca.com
Glades Plaza / 2200 Glades Rd., Suite 506
Boca Raton 33431 / (561) 338-0656
OPEN: Mon.-Sat. 10-5:30

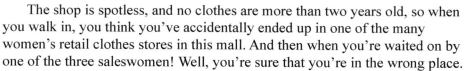

This is probably Boca Raton's most high-end consignment – indeed, one of the most upscale in Southeast Florida. And they've been voted the #1 consignment shop by Boca Raton Magazine for almost 10 years in a row.

The shop is spotless, and no clothes are more than two years old, so when you walk in, you think you've accidentally ended up in one of the many women's retail clothes stores in this mall. And then when you're waited on by one of the three saleswomen! Well, you're sure that you're in the wrong place.

But you're not. This is a super high-end women's clothing and accessories shop. In season they even carry a small rack of, never-been-worn-looking furs, rare to see that in a Florida consignment shop. Behind glass are the very upscale designer handbags, plus the selection of real as well as costume jewelry, with names you may know like David Yurman, Judith Ripka, Stephen Dweck, and others. You won't find too many sale items but there's always at least one rack in the back.

If you don't believe one shoe can change your life,
ask Cinderella

SHE'S SO SHABBY

shessoshabby.com
1720 NW 1st Ave. / Boca Raton 33432 / (954) 655-3937
OPEN: Tues.-Sat. 11-5.

If you don't know whether you like shabby chic because you don't know what it is, the owner and creator here, Jodi, describes it as "grandma's furniture painted for today's shabby style." This charming 3,000 square foot showroom– it used to be in Deerfield – has hand painted shabby chic furniture. But besides that, they offer many delightful one-of-a-kind items to decorate your cottage style home.

This is a unique showroom, painting studio & warehouse all in one. When the bay door is up, you will be brought back into time while listening to old time music on their 1965 Wurlitzer jukebox, strolling through their hand painted vintage furniture, frames, windows & salvage.

They can also custom paint pieces… and alternately, "shabby" your treasured pieces and most kitchen cabinets.

They're also the authorized retailer for American Paint Company Paints & Products.

So, if you are looking for that repurposed, recycled, reloved, reshabbified piece of furniture, you will find it here! Do you have your own treasured but unfinished piece? Then learn how to paint it in their workshops. All in all, this place is – as they say – not too shabby.

CHILDREN'S CLOTHES & FURNITURE (CONSIGNMENT)

SHOW & TELL CONSIGNMENTS & BOUTIQUE

www.showandtellconsign.com / Facebook: Show And Tell Consignments
260 N. Dixie Hwy. / Boca Raton 33432 / (561) 391-1117
OPEN: Mon. 12-5; Tues.- Fri. 10-5:30; Sat. 10:30–5; Sun. 12-4

When you walk in and see the stunning clothing and accessories, you think you've seen it all. But as you proceed to the next room, it opens up into a kid land. An adult land, actually, because it's a joy for both of you. Show & Tell is well situated, near Mizner Park, one block north of Palmetto Park Road. It's the largest (4,000 square feet - wow!) children's consignment shop in Boca, actually the largest for miles around. I don't have children but I would almost want one just to outfit in the great children's clothes in this shop.

This huge emporium carries new and gently-used brand name items, starting from pregnancy garments right through to preteen. They also sell harder-to-find school uniforms, dance and sports gear, dress-up and costume clothes, gifts, and baby shower presents. So come here and in one place, you'll find all you need in clothes, furniture (strollers, cribs, bedding, plush outdoor pieces) baby gear, maternity, books, movies and toys, like Pack N Plays dolls, and battery-operated cars. And best of all, there's always a sale!

CLOTHES & MISCELLANEOUS (THRIFT)

TRI COUNTY HUMANE SOCIETY THRIFT SHOP

http://tricountyhumane.org/thrift-shop
Plum Tree Center / 3350 NW 2nd Ave. / Boca Raton 33431 / (561) 338-4770
OPEN: Tues.-Sat. 10-4

The only thing wrong with the Tri County Humane Society thrift shop is that it's hard to find. They've moved to Plum Tree Center, between Spanish River Road and 28th Street.

Once you do find it, you'll learn that it's full of merchandise wherever you turn. It's better than most thrifts of this type because of the vintage clothes plus higher-end designer labels mixed in with everything else. Best of all, every dime you spend here supports a wonderful no-kill not-for-profit pet shelter that serves southeast Florida.

This place is also great for people looking for merchandise with pets on them, like dogs or cats on china or mugs. They're often donated by pet lovers who already have too many cat plates, or can't get their dog to climb those dog steps someone bought them for Christmas.

CHILDREN'S CLOTHES & FURNITURE (CONSIGNMENT)

WILL & EMMA'S CLOSET

www.willandemmascloset.com / Facebook: WILL & EMMAS CLOSET
Delmar Shopping Village 7126 Beracasa Way / Boca Raton 33433
(561) 353-5437 (KIDS)
OPEN: Mon.–Fri. 10-7; Sat. Sun. 10-4

Will & Emma's Closet has won many awards for outfitting everyone from infants through teens, and one step inside and you can see why. This two-part children's shop (they also have a furniture shop at 7088 but you have to walk here to get there) has everything child-related. That includes dazzling party dresses, charming suits, and brand new separates for children which have all been highly discounted. Look carefully at the clothes and the price tags dangling from them and you'll see that this shop deserves all their accolades. And another bonus: they often get new clothes in that have been acquired from children's shops that have gone out of business. To keep updated on sales, merchandise coming in, etc, follow them on Facebook.

CONSIGNMENT SHOP NEARBY: COCOBLUE. (See p. 8)

HOME DÉCOR (CONSIGNED & RETAIL)

ZANNA JANE'S WEST BOCA

www.zannajanes.com.
11419E W. Palmetto Park Rd. / Boca Raton 33428 / (561) 961-4341
OPEN: Tues.-Sat 10-6

They have seven different rooms, some of which are heavy on jewelry, with vintage and antique their specialty. It's mostly consigned, although they do have some retail jewelry tossed in as well. Mainly, though, the rooms are filled with lots of home décor, sometimes a bit different from what you'll find elsewhere. "We take the most unusual items," says Julie, the owner. "If someone comes in with something you can't find anywhere else, we take it." But, she added, they don't take clothing.

On Saturdays they serve tea and cookies from 11-5.

One more thing: how did they get their name? "Zanna Jane was supposed to be the name of my baby girl but I had two boys instead. And that's it. No more. So I named the store Zanna Jane because now she's my baby girl," said Julie.

THRIFT SHOP NEARBY: At 11427 W. Palmetto Park Road, is a GOODWILL AT LOGGER'S RUN so run here first.

BARGAIN SAVING TIP: If you want better clothes, go to a consignment shop. If you want better bargains, go to a thrift shop. People bring clothes good enough to sell to a consignment shop, and they receive a percentage of what the store received in the sale, usually 50%. People give away clothes to thrift shops so usually they're not as good as what they could consign for money. Unless it's a "quality thrift," like the one above, which carries better merchandise.

SPECIAL SHOPPING TOUR
THREE BLOCKS OF THRIFT-CONSIGNMENT-ANTIQUE & VINTAGE SHOPS IN DELRAY

Start at: **BETHESDA BARGAIN BOX**, (See p. 26). It's a thrift shop at 12 NE 5th Ave. which is also southbound Federal Hwy. Next door at 10 NE 5th Avenue is another thrift shop.

If you continue west one block on Atlantic and turn left at 4th Ave., at #10 is a women's consignment shop, **SECOND TIME AROUND** (See p. 38)

Or, go East on Atlantic Avenue to **A BLAST FROM THE PAST** at 777 East Atlantic, next to Chico's. (See p. 25)

FOR MORE SHOPS IN DELRAY, SEE BELOW.

MEN'S & WOMEN'S VINTAGE CLOTHING & ACCESSORIES

A BLAST FROM THE PAST
777 E Altantic Ave. (next to Chico's) / Delray Beach 33483 / (561) 272-8290
OPEN: Mon.-Fri. 12:30-8; Sat. 12:30-9:30; Sun. 12:30-8

To give you an idea of how unusual this store is, what you pay is determined by the roll of the dice. The owner, Dee, has a fuzzy die, and when you check out, she tosses it. Depending on whether it lands on 5, 10 or 15, that's the percentage off you receive.

Much is unique–not just that–and often very rare here. You'll find original Puccis. Guccis. Hermes. Miriam Haskell jewelry. Perfect condition handbags. Often vintage, but some of the merchandise is new. And what's also unusual is they've sold contemporary bags, like Chanels, at the same time as vintage Chanels.

I was dating a transvestite and my mother said:
"Marry him. You'll double your wardrobe."

– Joan Rivers

HOME DÉCOR & JEWELRY

ALEXANDER'S DELRAY DESIGN

www.adelraydesign.com

777 E Atlantic Ave., Suite B5 / Delray Beach 33483 /(561) 303-1456

OPEN: Mon.-Sun. 10-6

The original Delray Beach Antique Mall has moved around quite a bit, but their part owner, Alexander, seems to have finally settled here in this artistic mall a couple of blocks east of Atlantic & Federal. Although it's a bit off the beaten track, you can find it easily because it's a few doors away from Chico's.

This place should also prove popular because the jewelry – some of it stunning – and that along with the art are nicely priced. You'll also find more globally inspired items—Alexander, an artist and a designer is a Scot – than at many antique, art and home décor outlets.

Some of what is here is new, some old, some consigned, others purchased outright, sometimes from abroad. There's also a small amount of clothes – even for dogs – some made by Alexander herself.

Upstairs on the second door they teach art in what is the largest art colony for miles around. They have a lot of events here, so keep up by going to their website

CLOTHES, FURNITURE & MISCELLANEOUS (QUALITY THRIFT)

BETHESDA BARGAIN BOX

12 NE 5th Ave. (southbound Federal Hwy.) /
Delray Beach 33483
(561) 278-2401

OPEN: Mon.-Fri. 10-5; Sat. 10-2

PARKING: Going south, keep an eye open for a small parking lot on the right

before the store. It says "Bethesda Bargain Box" on the wall.

"Bargain Box" is an apt name for this popular Delray thrift, although the word "box" might lead you to believe that it's small, which Bethesda Bargain Box definitely is not. It's one of the largest thrifts between Boca Raton and Jupiter, and there are many different sections to explore in this "box." The large main room, filled with boutique clothes, shoes, lingerie, children's toys, glassware and home décor is worth the trip alone. Especially since the prices are so good they could best be described as double take, particularly when there's a sale of some sort, which frequently occurs.

Continue on through a winding alleyway of photo frames, art, books (probably the largest collection of books in this area outside of a real library) until you reach "The Barn." It's filled with lower-end bric-a-brac and linens, and mostly not-so-new furniture, but at sensational prices, especially the outdoor furniture. To top it off, in the corner they also have golf clubs for $3-$5, and golf shoes for $5-$9.

This shop has been in existence since 1962 and is expertly managed by Michelle Esposito, and her Mom is often at the counter. Michelle says they offer "boutique-style shopping where everything is sized and organized for you." She's right.

FLEA MARKET

BIG APPLE SHOPPING BAZAAR

http://thebigappleshoppingbazaar.com
www.facebook.com/TheBigAppleShoppingBazaar
5283 W. Atlantic Ave. / Delray Beach 33484 / (561) 499-9935
OPEN: Wed.-Sat. 10-5:30; Sun. 11-5

What can you say about an indoor flea market? That they've got lots of stuff? That you'll probably buy something cheaper than you would in a regular store? That you can find a lot of things under one roof? OK, I said it. And it's true here.

This mid-sized flea market (60 booths) is unexceptional and unexceptionable. Sure you'll find something you didn't even know you needed and at a reasonable price. So, if you're nearby, try it, you'll like it. But to go any distance, you'll use up in gas what you save on your purchase. Better still, use up more gas and go to FESTIVAL (SAMPLE ROAD) FLEA MARKET. (See p. 139)

CHARITY CONSIGNMENT

955 S. Congress Ave. Suite 103
Delray Beach 33445 / (561) 455-2559
OPEN: Tues. Wed. Fri. Sat. 1-5; Thurs. 10-7

It's easy to see why the readers of the Forum voted Charity Consignment the Number One consignment shop in "Best of Delray," because you'll take one step onto the floor – and be floored. The main room is filled with so many fun and wonderful things you don't even know where to begin. Do you go left to the large second room, and continue from there to the two small art galleries? Or should you go right, to the "Baby Boomer Boutique," which promises "Designer Deals from Head to Heels," and more areas heavily stocked with clothes and accessories– including men's.

And just when you think you've seen everything, you spot more. Flamingo pillows. Crutches. Jeweled guitars. Books. Couches. Since there's so much space – 8,000 square feet– they can carry some large furniture pieces here. Some of what's on the floor is consigned; some donated. But plan on spending a lot of time and having a lot of fun as you look through things you've never seen before.

Two other pluses: the money goes to Charity Consignment, which locates and leases single family homes for working single parents with minor children.

Plus they offer a free pick up for donations.

As exciting as what's in here (and that includes Freddi, their malti-poo) are the prices. The pre-owned inventory often comes with thrift store prices. "We try to be upscaley but without upscaley prices," says Richard Kheel, who co-owns the place with his wife Merry. Merry's a great name for an owner of this place, because you are absolutely guaranteed to have a merry time here.

*"Too many people spend money they haven't earned,
to buy things they don't want, to impress people they don't like."*
– Will Rogers

CHILDREN'S CLOTHES & FURNITURE (CONSIGNMENT)

CONSIGN-A-KIDS

Facebook: consign.akids
Linton International Plaza / 660 Linton Blvd., Suite 101B
Delray Beach 33444 / (561) 276-9798
OPEN: Tues.-Sat. 10-4

As soon as you walk in and see the photos of all the children the owner has outfitted, you realize the love and attention Alba Francesca Arts has poured into this store for almost two decades. That's probably one reason that year after year, they're named one of the best consignment shop for children by prestige magazines like *Parents*.

The other reason is the merchandise and the extent of it. This two-room consigned and new merchandise shop – the latter at the same price as the consignment–carries not only the expected children's clothes but also costumes, and even kids' ice skating outfits. Plus, girls and boys from birth to the age of 14 are wardrobed right down to their feet in the "shoe salon" alcoves in back. A second room to the right has cribs, children's furniture, and gifts.

FURNITURE & HOME DÉCOR (CONSIGNMENT)

CONSIGN DESIGN HOME FURNISHINGS

www.consigndesigndelray.com
14560 S. Military Trail / Delray Beach 33480 / (561) 496–0006
OPEN: Mon.-Sat. 10-6

This extremely popular home accessories consignment store in Delray Square has been voted the best consignment in Delray for five years in a row, based on ballots by the residents.

Oddly, for the past five years I didn't understand its popularity. I went in a couple of times and was not overly impressed since the selection was small. But everywhere people would tell me that this was one of their favorite shops.

But when I went again recently, I discovered something amazing: there are two huge back rooms that I didn't know about. Inside is much much more of what you find up front: beautiful furniture and home accents. Great prices. Wonderful art. Lamps, glassware, dishes, rugs, chandeliers, and antiques. "We like to take unusual things in good condition," said one of the salespeople. Maybe that explains what makes it so unusual – and so good.

FURNITURE SHOP NEARBY: AAA CONSIGNMENT at 13900 Jog Road (561 613-7474) is a large furniture shop. They carry a lot of heavy pieces, such as couches and dining sets, chairs (including recliners), and a small amount of bedroom sets. Throughout, you'll spot a number of attractive small gift and home décor items that make going through the store fun. The larger pieces aren't inexpensive but the small ones are. Open Mon.-Sat.10-5:30; Sun.12-5.

HOW TO SPOT A GOOD THRIFT SHOP

How do you tell if a garment you want to buy is, well, too thrifty? You look at the label to see how worn it is; you look at the pockets to see how stretched it is; and you take a sniff to see how smelly it is.

Says Dan Demicell, a top resale marketing consultant "When you walk into a thrift shop, it shouldn't smell like one," he said. "When you look around it shouldn't look like one. It should be clean, orderly and what you buy should be worth what you pay for it," he stressed.

MISCELLANEOUS HOME DÉCOR (CONSIGNMENT)

DECORATOR ROW
1550 N. Federal Hwy. / Delray Beach 33483
(561) 303-1456 & (561) 278-5999
OPEN: Mon.-Sun. 10-7

This small easy-to-miss mall (it's between the large Habitat thrift shop called RESTORE and a large spa), but don't miss it if you're looking for used, vintage and consignment home décor at a really good price. There are two owners for the five small rooms, a few interconnected.

Several of the shops go under the name of CURIOUSLY BEAUTIFUL (owned by Juliana) and another (in the middle) is called THEN AND NOW CONSIGNMENTS owned by Elaine. That's all you need to know – except that on weekends, they have a flea market where about 8 dealers bring their wares and they set up in front of these shops.

Don't get confused about who owns what and what it's called. Just come. The five small shops carry everything (small furniture, jewelry, lighting, furnishings, antiques, art, home décor, china, collectibles, and more) and their already low prices are often even lower since they're open to negotiation. "We don't carry junk but we don't sell $2,000 items either," said Juliana who likes to keep things moving. "This is not a museum. We get things every day." At those prices and with that merchandise, you can see why the items move.

Novices, as well as experienced dealers, are sure to find something. In fact, Scott Simmons, who writes the fascinating "Look What We Found" column in the *Palm Beach Post* (don't miss it), featured a rare resin inlaid box with a beautiful red bird on it he found there – for only $24. "This is the first time I ever have seen a Couroc box," he wrote. As the old cliché goes, expect the unexpected.

WOMEN'S CLOTHING & ACCESSORIES (CONSIGNMENT)

FRUGAL FASHIONISTA

Facebook: Frugal Fashionista Resale Boutique
825 N. Federal Hwy., (or NE 6th Ave) / Delray
Beach 33435 / (561) 865-7857
OPEN: Tues.-Sat. 11-5

One block North of George Bush Blvd. is a resale shop where the owner, Amber Ortoll, buys women's apparel outright. But not from you. "I don't take traditional consignment with people coming in with bags. I have 5 or 6 girls who hunt thrift stores from Miami to North Palm Beach cherry-picking the best for me."

Sounds like a fun job for them! And it helps the customer because the store then stocks what is needed. "I'm a style schizophrenic because I like a lot of things," Amber admitted. But what's here is attractive and very very well priced. Almost nothing is more than $20 and a lot is less than that. For example, a pair of Stuart Weitzmans in good condition for $20. An Alberto Mikali blouse (normally $120 at Nordstrom) for $20. There are lots of hats and shoes here but not much jewelry. Usually you can find a $5 rack by the register.

"When women are depressed, they eat or go shopping. Men invade another country. It's a whole different way of thinking."
– Elayne Boosler

VINTAGE, CLOTHES & MISCELLANEOUS (THRIFT)

GOODWILL

www.gulfstreamgoodwill.com
1640 N. Federal Hwy / Delray Beach 33483 / (561) 278-3205
OPEN: Mon.-Sat. 9-8; Sun. 10-6

This was once an interesting Goodwill because they had a large multi-room vintage shop in the back, with its own entrance even. Most of what was in there looked old and ugly, but one man's old and ugly is another man's vintage.

Now, don't bother going to the back anymore because it is no more. Instead, we're left with a typical Goodwill and not a very good one at that.

RESTAURANT NEARBY: Ellie's 50's Diner. You can find a bit of neon nostalgia at Ellie's 50's Diner and Flamingo Room and you'll know you're at the right restaurant – which, by the way, only takes cash – when you see the pink '58 Chevrolet parked outside. Inside, waitresses wear pink poodle skirts, and the menu items are named for the 50's. An authentic-looking (OK, bizarre) jukebox plays 50's era music, and that means plenty of Elvis. Hearing (and seeing since he's all around) so much of him can leave you all shook up, but, hey, that's when your heartache begins. 2410 N. Federal Hwy. (561 276-1570)

WOMEN'S CLOTHING & ACCESSORIES (CONSIGNMENT & NEW)

GUTSY BOUTIQUE

13800 Jog Rd. / Delray Beach 33446
(561) 364-4888
OPEN: Mon.-Sat. 10-5

About a year and a half ago, this shop was transplanted from Boynton to the west part of Delray, where there are far fewer consignment shops than over on the east part of the town.

So it takes guts to go in a different place – Boynton too had a scarcity of women's consignment shops – which may be why it's called (drum roll) Gutsy Boutique.

This turns out to be a lovely woman's clothes-and-accessories shop that carries both new and hardly-used clothes. They have a separate section here for petites, and a super clearance rack of about half off, along with a $5 rack in the front of the store. And for the Chico-philes, there's four racks of consigned Chico's.

They don't divide the new from the resale. Since both look the same – the difference is that the new have tags and are reduced slightly less than the resale – perhaps it doesn't matter. And the new may be greatly reduced anyway, such as the earrings she was selling recently for $25 each that she had purchased from a closing shop for over $100 a piece. They also don't have a set time to reduce things. "Periodically I'll run around and mark things off," says the owner, Rochelle Love.

What does matter is that this is a very pleasant place that services an area that had needed it and it's packed, really packed with clothes. It will take a long time to go through it and you'll enjoy yourself doing it.

The owner also makes unusual jewelry that she sells – and wears – and you can also buy a T-shirt here saying "Gutsy," if you want to advertise the store, or your spirit.

WOMEN'S SPECIAL OCCASION CLOTHING & ACCESSORIES (CONSIGNMENT & NEW)

GUTSY GOWNS
13800 Jog Rd. / Delray Beach 33446 / (561) 364-4888
OPEN: By appointment only

In the same shopping center (San Marco), a few doors away, the owner of GUTSY BOUTIQUE (see above) has opened a second shop called Gutsy Gowns. Here, she sells formal, cocktail and special occasion clothes, fancy shoes, fancy handbags, and fancy jewelry. Fancy that!

The shop is stocked (not nearly as crowded as her sister shop) with everything for going out on special occasions, including specialized gowns, such as wedding dresses (she has a few there), plus mother-of-the-bride dresses, bridesmaid gowns, and more. "We're not Chanel," said the salesperson. "Someone can buy a lovely gown here for under $200." She was right, although there was an interesting story behind a gown there for $429 – an $8,000 spectacular-looking silk organza wedding dress with a beaded satin bodice and matching beaded jacket.

The owner had never worn it. When she consigned it here, she commented that the gown cost her a lot less money than the marriage would have cost her had she gone through it. Sounds like an interesting story.

Looks like an interesting place.

SHOP NEARBY: If you're looking for couches, chairs, paintings, and large pieces, you should come first to AAA – no, not the car company but a furniture consignment liquidator. "We buy everything from soup to nuts from estates," says the owner of this huge 5,500 square feet large furniture and home décor store several doors down from GUTSY BOUTIQUE.

What makes for especially interesting shopping here is that over on the left when you come in, are rows of smaller items from crystal to knickknacks and a lot of fun things for very little money. 13900 Jog Road (561) 613-7474. OPEN: Mon-Sat. 10-5; Sun. 12-5.

CLOTHING AND HOME DÉCOR (OUTLET)

HARVEY'S ON FIRST & THE SNAPPY TURTLE OUTLETS

www.snappy-turtle.com
102 NE 1st Ave. / Delray Beach 33444 / (561) 276-3308
OPEN: Mon.-Sat. 10-5

Once, The Snappy Turtle Outlets – three Delray Beach shops called Snappy Turtle, Love Shack and Harvey's on First – were in a beautiful outlet on George Bush Boulevard in Delray Beach. Now, they've closed the complex, but thankfully the sale continues on. You can find it in five rooms on the second floor of Harvey's On First. The three stores are still offering the same great deals – at least 50% and often more on the stores' wares, namely women's clothes, some men's and children's, and a bit of home interior products as well. Love Shack & Snappy Turtle reduces their sales clothes by 50% and sends them to the Harvey's on First shop.

WHAT IS A VINTAGE SHOP?

Vintage shops sell older merchandise, almost always in better condition and more stylish than older merchandise in thrift shops (unless you're lucky). They're usually sold in specialized vintage shops, but you may find some in estate sales, and garage sales, which are often outdoors. Then there are rummage sales, whose merchandise is usually quite cheap, and... oh what the heck. If it has the word "sale" go to it.

KISMET OF DELRAY: VINTAGE AND DESIGNER CLOTHING

www.kismetvintage.com / Facebook: kismet vintage
Pineapple Grove Arts District / 157 NE 2nd Ave.
Delray Beach 33444 / (561) 865-7895
OPEN: Mon.-Fri. 11-6; Sat. 10-8; Sun. 11-4

Here's something different. Kismet of Delray trades clothes, giving you 40% on the spot for what you bring in that they accept. While trading clothes here may be nice, shopping may be even more rewarding. You can find good recycled vintage clothing in this relatively lean uncluttered place. An extremely pleasant and happy-to-please husband and wife, Aly and Lee Sutherland, own this eco-friendly vintage shop, featuring many designer labels. For example, they had a man's Robert Graham shirt (normally in the $200+ area) for $60. An even more expensive Etro men's shirt was one-third less than at Neiman Marcus.

MIMI'S CHEST

Facebook: Mimis Chest
400 Gulfstream Blvd. / Delray 33444 / (561) 271-3937
OPEN: Tues.–Sat. 12:30–5

The "recycled treasures" in this "gift shop with furniture"– as owner Mimi Rizek refers to it–isn't really a thrift or consignment shop. What do you call a fabulous little house, overflowing with the most marvelously fun décor and gifts that she has purchased and is now selling at a low, low price? A great find.

I lost count of how many small rooms and alcoves there are– I think 11 including 3 bathrooms (and what's in there is for sale too so that counts). If you're here with a friend, you'll find yourself constantly shouting to them "Hey, look at this" – and the prices are so low you may then argue as to which of you can buy it. (And a note to pet lovers: there are many wonderful dog and cat gifts here.) To find it (a bit difficult the first time, but you will be back), turn at the Dunkin' Donuts on Federal, and you're on Gulfstream Boulevard. Go about a block and you'll see the little house on the left.

NEARBY: WALMART at 3625 Federal Highway.

HOME DÉCOR (BEACHY)

NEST

nestdelray.com; https://www.facebook.com/NestOfdelray
817 NE 6th Ave. / Delray Beach 33483 / (561) 900-7181
OPEN: Mon.-Sat. 10:30-5

The only reason to come here is that you're right next door visiting the fabulous FRUGAL FASHIONISTA (see p. 31) or you like really country beachy stuff. There's not much here, and the parking for it is grim. There are a couple of spaces slightly south of the shop, but then you have to back your car into heavy traffic to get out.... nothing here is worth an accident.

They carry vintage, (no clothes, tiny amount of jewelry), along with refinished and custom furniture and home décor. Often some good pillows.

You can get a feel for what's here by going to their website or Facebook page (see above) but the items look a lot better there. Besides, it's a lot easier "getting around" online than in this small cluttered shop – and you don't have to park! But as with all these places, if you're looking, or just browsing, you never know what you'll find.

SHOP NEARBY: Around the corner, at 901 George Bush Boulevard, is GREAT STUFF PREVIOUSLY OWNED. There are no bargains in this super upscale home décor and art consignment shop, although there are a few small items for under $25. A few. Very few. Most of it is quite expensive – but beautiful.

They have three large rooms and some alleys, and it's easy to get lost when trying to leave because you have to work your way back to the only entrance. But it's a wonderful place to get lost in! (561) 243-0010 Mon.-Sat. 10-4.

FURNITURE & HOME GOODS (THRIFT)

RESTORE (HABITAT FOR HUMANITY)

www.habitat.org/restores
1900 N. Federal Hwy. / Delray Beach 33483 / (561) 455-4441
OPEN: Tues.-Sat. 10-6; Sun. 11-5

It really is Christmas in July, June, January or whenever you come here, because they have a special section of Christmas-related merchandise and the area is filled all year round.

But Restore is Christmas in July because it truly is a gift: a large (bigger than the one in Boca), well-lit, clean store with fabulous prices and a lot of really nice offerings. Yes, mostly furniture, but enough else – a small selection of clothes, books, paintings, gifts, appliances – to make it a worthwhile stop for anyone and everyone. ("It's like a clean Goodwill with furniture," said one customer.)

We all have the image of former President Jimmy Carter building houses for Habitat for Humanity. But this place is so much more than just a thrift shop for people looking for furniture or home appliances and even things like doors, sconces, hurricane shutters, decorator items, household construction pieces. And what you buy here helps a number of charities that help the underprivileged, mostly looking for housing.

OTHER RESTORE/HABITAT FOR HUMANITY SHOPS IN SOUTHEAST FLORIDA

272 S. Dixie Hwy. / Boca Raton 33432 / (561) 362-7284

1635 N Old Dixie Hwy. / Jupiter 33469 / (561) 743-3660

2299 NW 77 Terrace / Miami 33147 / (305) 637-4913

6831 N. Military Trail / West Palm Beach 33407 / (561) 253-2290

JACK THE RIPPER IN DELRAY BEACH

Driving toward the ocean on Atlantic, you'll find an interesting building/restaurant with a connection to Jack the Ripper and Winston Churchill. And the food is great as well!

The Blue Anchor British Pub was an authentic 1864 Anglican drinking establishment that was dismantled and shipped piece-by-piece across the ocean to its current spot at 804 Atlantic Ave.

During its earlier incarnation, when it was on famed Chancery Lane in London, two of its patrons were ultimately victims of the Ripper. A third loyal customer (but obviously not a visitor to the pub at the same time) was Winston Churchill.

Another regular was a woman murdered in the pub by her jealous husband. It is said by some that her ghost continues to haunt the halls of the Blue Anchor. If so, it may be the first ghost to ever cross the Atlantic.

WOMEN'S CLOTHING & ACCESSORIES (CONSIGNMENT)

SECOND TIME AROUND

Facebook: Second Time Around Delray
10 SE 4th Ave. / Delray Beach 33483
(561) 278-0493
OPEN: Mon.-Fri. 10-5; Sat.-Sun. 10-4

This ladies' consignment boutique–the only women's consignment shop in Delray– was first established in 1980. It's now twice the size since they recently purchased the shop next door. So if you recall a tiny little shop next to a store selling tiny little doll house accessories, wait till you see Second Time Around now. They still carry a large assortment of consigned casual, professional, and evening clothes plus jewelry, designer shoes, and handbags. And now the new shop will be carrying furniture and home accents. Prices are often reduced to keep merchandise moving, and there's a large sale rounder in the back that you won't want to miss.

Rule of life: if the shoe fits, it's ugly.

HOW SNEAKY

Yes, sneakers got their name because they were, well, sneaky. With their rubber soles, people could sneak around without giving their presence away. But what about some of the names for sneaker? For example, does Adidas really stand for "All Day I Dream About Soccer" (there's also a dirtier version) as some believe.

Not according to Mental Floss magazine, which did an article on the origin of sneaker names. For example, Clyde (as in Puma Clyde) got its name because Walt Frasier, for whom the shoe was originally designed, often dressed like the famous bank robber, Clyde Barrow.

Keds should have been "peds" from the Latin word for "feet." But someone else already owned the name so they changed it to Keds. And Brooks was supposed to be named after its owner, but he wanted a less ethnic name and anlicized his wife's maiden name, Bruchs. Can you imagine a successful pair of sneakers if they had been called Morris Goldenberg's?

Jupiter & Juno Beach

(NOT TO SCALE)

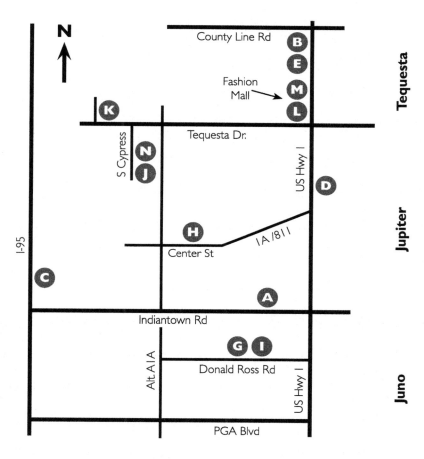

A ..... A Star's Closet (p. 40)

B ..... Angels in the Attic (p. 92)

C ..... Antique Mall at Sims Creek (p. 40)

D ..... Classic Furnishings (p. 92)

E ..... Forever Young (p. 93)

F ..... Habitat for Humanity (p. 41)

G ..... Hospice Resale Shop North (p. 41)

H .... Jupiter Medical Center (p. 42)

I .... Ladies Closet (p. 43)

J .... Man Cave (p. 43)

K .... Pennies for Heaven (p. 93)

L ..... Snooty Hooty's (p. 94)

M .... Tequesta Stock Exchange (p. 94)

N .... The Good Stuff (p. 44)

WOMEN'S CLOTHING & ACCESSORIES (CONSIGNMENT)

A STAR'S CLOSET

http://astarscloset.com / Facebook: A Stars Closet
Concourse Village / 75 E. Indiantown Rd., #503 / Jupiter 33477
(561) 747-0240
OPEN: Mon.-Fri. 10-5:30; Sat. 10-5

A stylish upscale consignment shop with cutting edge clothes, and to top it off, it's located in an easy-to-find mall. Claudette Cerro, the owner, who works with her daughter, Tina, has filled her shop with trendy accessories and attractive designer women's apparel, such as colorful Lilly Pulitzer and classic St. John knits.

In addition, the two showcases of unique jewelry, both vintage and new, had many attractive pieces. Put this on your must-try-out list and it will become one of your regular haunts.

SHOPS NEARBY: Two discount stores, T.J. MAXX and ROSS DRESS FOR LESS are in the same mall, at #400 and #300 respectively.

ANTIQUE MALL

ANTIQUE MALL AT SIMS CREEK

http://simscreekantiques.com
1695 W. Indiantown Rd. / Jupiter 33458
(561) 747-6785
OPEN: Tues.-Sat. 11-6

If you want to get a feel for what's at this antique mall, plenty is pictured on their website, along with the prices. This 5,000-square-foot mall across from Home Depot, featuring more than 200 booths, is one of the largest antique malls in Palm Beach County. It's probably the most popular in the northern sector of the county too. It has been in operation for 15 years, and its success and inviting atmosphere owe a lot to its welcoming owners, Olga Pawela and Fiona Nichols. You have to go there in person to see the charming mixture of kitschy collectibles – like kittens dancing. There is a nice mix of formal gowns, contemporary and vintage, to go along with the vintage accessories, all displayed with a scattering of newer high-end garments that include an occasional hot designer like Louis Vuitton, Gucci, and Coach.

THRIFT SHOP NEARBY: GOODWILL JUPITER SUPERSTORE is at 1280 W. Indiantown Rd.

HOME GOODS & CLOTHES (THRIFT)

HABITAT FOR HUMANITY

1635 N. Old Dixie Hwy. / Jupiter 33469 /(561) 743-3660
OPEN: Mon.-Wed. 9-4; Thurs. 9-5; Fri. Sat. 9-4

There are several Habitat for Humanities Thrift Shop (see pp. 36 & 37) but they're not anything like this one. In fact, few thrift shops are like this one. It's in a very attractive stand-alone building and it's humongous. And fabulous

As you walk around you find more and more rooms – the best is the back one, the Boutique. Most thrift shop "boutiques" really aren't, and they may only have a few worthwhile garments. But this really was a boutique with a lot of better garments. And the large room before it, with men and women's clothes and accessories wasn't bad. Not to mention that there are two book nooks, and even a separate room just for linens.

Up front are some few more expensive items but still well priced: a Tiffany key holder with the box for $95; a largish cute Swarovski Dalmatian dog for $88. The front room holds several better gifts and home décor in a couple of glass cases, some forgettable jewelry, and several large couches and pieces of furniture priced so low as to be almost ridiculous. Make this one your favorite Habitat; make it one of your favorite thrift shops.

CLOTHES, FURNITURE & MISCELLANEOUS (QUALITY THRIFT)

HOSPICE: RESALE SHOP NORTH

www.hpbc.com/resale / Plaza La Mer 863 Donald Ross Rd.
Juno Beach 33408 / (561) 624-5495
OPEN: Mon.-Sat. 10-5

A lot of good merchandise is ready to leave here and find a home – yours – in this spacious, cheerful, five-room thrift shop. You could easily buy something from any section. That's especially true of the two ample-sized rooms of furniture, which feature particularly attractive unused-looking couches, chairs, and tables. Then too, the clothes sections for both men and women are more than what you'd find in a typical (or inexpensive) consignment shop, but with cheaper prices.

DON'T MISS: There are two small easily-missed back areas – one to the left behind the women's clothes, the other in back of the linens in the main room. They contain miscellany and well-priced high-quality men's clothes,

CONSIGNMENT SHOP NEARBY: LADIES CLOSET (formerly a consignment shop called Off Price Boutique) is at 849 Donald Ross Rd., in the same mall a few doors over. (See p. 43.)

CLOTHES & MISCELLANEOUS (THRIFT)

JUPITER MEDICAL CENTER THRIFT SHOP

www.jupitermed.com/thrift-shop
205 Center St. / Jupiter 33458 / (561) 746-1601
OPEN: Mon.-Fri. 9:30-4; Sat. 9-2

Toward the back of the Jupiter Medical Center Thrift Shop was a rack of St. Johns.

Wait a minute? St. Johns in a thrift shop? Well, many pleasant surprises await you here. In addition to the typical thrift goods, they also sell musical instruments, cars, and boats. This unusually large, clean thrift is definitely worth a visit because of its great prices for attractive clothes, decorative accessories, and household goods. A small separate section in the middle

---

WHERE TOM CRUISED...

How do people feel about buying clothes worn by celebrities? Not only do they want them, but the great unwashed wants the great, unwashed. Meaning that the average person wants clothes that famous people have worn without their being laundered or anything of them taken away.

"People want them dirty lest Brad Pitt or Barack Obama's fairy dust fall(s) off," says Paul Bloom, the author of "How Pleasure Works."

If they want this "aura" on the clothes (or in Tom Cruise's case, the body thetans or alien beings he has paid millions to Scientology to try to eradicate,) how do people feel about wearing clothes that have been worn, say, by killers? Ewwww. People told that a sweater was worn by a murderer wouldn't wear it.

contains teenage clothes, which are often hard to find at thrifts because they're generally mixed in with the other garments, if they have them at all. A large men's section is to the left.

DON'T MISS: If you look straight ahead, you'll see what appears to be a room of books. But when you enter it, you'll see a large area to the right containing mainly household goods and goodies.

WOMEN'S CLOTHING & ACCESSORIES (CONSIGNMENT)

LADIES CLOSET
48 Donald Ross Rd. / Juno Beach 33408 / (561) 223-2623
OPEN: Tues.-Sat. 10-5

It's not an attractive-looking place with its rows of clothes on metal racks and its diminished décor. But don't let that fool you. There are bargains to be had and attractive goods to examine, and it's just a few steps from one of the best thrift shops in the whole upper county, so you certainly should come here as well. Besides, it's run by a mother and daughter (Rovena and Tina) who are new to this and barely holding on, and they need all the help they can get so they're not lost in the far end of this mall.

Once inside, you'll find that it's pleasant, spread out, and you can walk comfortably around admiring the high-end —and affordable— very attractive, almost new-looking designer merchandise which is resale, not consignment. A trip to Ladies Choice and to the excellent Hospice thrift shop, which is just a few doors away is almost reason enough to make a trip to this mall.

THRIFT SHOP NEARBY: HOSPICE: RESALE SHOP NORTH is a few doors down. (See p. 41.)

MEN'S CLOTHES (CONSIGNMENT)

MAN CAVE
www.mancaveconsign.com
1535 Cypress Dr., Unit 2 / Jupiter 33469 / (561) 746-2283
OPEN: Tues.-Fri. 10-5; Sat. 10-2

Fortunately this doesn't look like a man cave, which one might expect to be dark, dirty and messy. Instead, this is a small bright shop featuring the too-often neglected area of better men's clothing, carrying (at considerably reduced prices) everything from jeans to evening wear, from low prices to well.... .

But a man can find more than just clothes here. The Man Cave also carries sporting equipment, memorabilia (sports pictures, posters, etc.,) electronics (pretested to make sure they work), tools, stuff for garages, boats, juke boxes, recliners, and more of what guys like.

They promise a "relaxed, fun and comfortable place where guys can go to be guys and shop for things that guys love." They also carry men's estate items, which some places don't want. And finally, they also cater to the cave woman searching for the right item for her cave man. So both sexes can feel very comfortable shopping here.

MEN'S CLOTHES (CONSIGNMENT)

THE GOOD STUFF
www.thegoodstuffconsignment.com &
www.facebook.com/thegoodstuffconsignment
1515 S. Cypress Dr. / Jupiter 33469 / (561) 746-8004
OPEN: Tues.-Fri. 10-5; Sat. 10-3

What on earth is Tiara Tuesday? If you are one of the many fans of The Good Stuff, a customer coming in wearing a tiara (men have done it too!) gets 10% off on his/her purchase. Now that's original.

But so is everything else, starting with the purple awning outside. Inside, the home décor, knickknacks, decoupage, and art are all charming, fun and kitschy. The new owner (alas, the girls are gone) Karen Williamson is a decorator known as the "Chic-o-rator" because she owns a decorating business called Chic My Shack. So she has a decorator's eye in what she chooses to be there. Indeed, part of the popularity of this slightly off-the-beaten track place is the unusual merchandise.

It's obvious everyone is having a good time here with their "good stuff." And they want to share their fun–as well as their good stuff–with their customers. So coming here is like visiting friends in a charming guest cottage who allow you to buy what's in their place. While accessorized in a tiara.

"Hats divide generally into three classes: offensive hats, defensive hats and shrapnel."

– Katherine Whitehorn

BEST NEW YORK (UPTOWN)
UPSCALE CONSIGNMENT & THRIFT SHOPS

ENCORE [www.encoreresale.com] the granddaddy of them all, is between 84th & 85th on the 2nd and 3rd floors of 1132 Madison Avenue.

BIS DESIGNER RESALE [www.bisbiz.com] is next door to Michaels at 1134 Madison, and it's also upstairs. Worth the steep climb up.

MICHAEL'S [www.michaelsconsignment.com] is between 79th and 80th at 1041 Madison Avenue, on the 2nd & 3rd floors. Don't miss the sale area way in back of the 3rd floor. You'll also sometimes find vintage and wedding gowns back there too.

LA BOUTIQUE RESALE [www.laboutiqueresale.com] is a few doors uptown from Michaels at 1045 Madison Ave. and they occupy the first and second floors.

DESIGNER RESALE CONSIGNMENT [www.designerresaleconsignment.com], at 324 East 81st Street. They have three attached shops, and you can find just about everything for women there. Next door, at 322 East 81st Street, is the men's upscale consignment shop.

A SECOND CHANCE 1111 Lexington Ave. between 77th and 78th Street, 2nd floor. [www.asecondchanceretail.com] The tacky neighborhood and unimpressive building gives you no idea how gorgeous (and expensive) the designer clothes, jewelry and handbags are in the second room. This place is Chanel heaven!

HOUSING WORKS (See Housingworks.Org For 12 Locations) The Happy Shopper is often unhappy with the Housing Works. While it was once wonderful, now they have too many shops for all the good merchandise, and they pull out the better merchandise to sell at their frequent special sales. Their salespeople often grab the best stuff (boo) and then you have to pay admission and stand on a long line waiting to get in to the special sales. (Boo hoo.)

The Soho branch (130 Crosby Street) is definitely the best, and their used bookstore (Bookstore Cafe at 126 Crosby) is a rarity in New York (or anywhere) now, and has far better bargains (and browsing) than their thrift shops.

Lake Worth - Lake Avenue

(NOT TO SCALE)

A.... Affluent Finds (p. 47)

B..... BKG Galleries (p. 48)

C.... Carousel Antique Center (p. 48)

D.... Charity Consignment Valentina's Treasures (p. 49)

E..... Fashion Exchange (p. 50)

F..... Palm Beach Home Interior Collection (p. 50)

G.... Sequels Boutique (p. 51)

LAKE WORTH – FOUR BLOCKS OF HOUSEHOLD DÉCOR, FURNITURE, GIFTS & WOMEN'S CONSIGNMENT SHOPS

A four-block stretch of Lake Avenue right off Dixie Highway is becoming the place for people looking to decorate their homes – and themselves. There are over a dozen consignment clothing, furniture, home décor shops, art, galleries, crafts, antique malls, and more here. There's also the Cultural Council of Palm Beach County in a beautiful Streamline Moderne building at 601 Lake Avenue, and they always have interesting exhibits, plus a shop that carries local fare.

WOMEN'S CLOTHES & ACCESSORIES (CONSIGNMENT)

AFFLUENT FINDS

www.affluentfinds.com
810 Lake Ave. / Lake Worth 33460
(561)588–7772
OPEN: Mon.-Sat. 11-6; Sun. 12-5

Affluent Finds is a fantastic women's consignment shop filled with designer labels. The owner, April Willis, handpicks each of the items and there is new merchandise constantly coming in.

Everything in the store is priced at about 75% off retail, and you can do better than that in the sale section. The clothes are in pristine condition, well organized and easy to find on the long racks – with a rolling rack in the center of the store with sale items in there. There's also an abundant amount of jewelry and sunglasses to the left and handbags to the right. The lovely window displays often contain the newest arrivals of fabulous high-end accessories and apparel, so don't miss it.

Affluent Finds appeals to a broader age base than many of these places, and carries something for every group, from the fun and fashionable, sporty teen, to the classic more sophisticated lady. Like the owner.

HOME ACCENTS SHOP NEARBY: A few doors down at 804 Lake Avenue is THE SUNFLOWER ROOM, another eclectic home décor and small furniture emporium. This space is extremely large, carrying everything from lighting to linens, specializing in wallpaper.

ANTIQUES & COLLECTIBLES

BKG GALLERIES

32 S. Dixie Hwy. / Lake Worth 33460 / (561) 533-7707
OPEN: Mon.- Wed. 10-5; Thurs. 10-8; Fri. & Sat. 10-5; Sun: 11-5

This is another place that can be hard to find – but once you do, it's worth it. You'll find it in back (slightly south) of Lake Avenue, but even after you enter the parking lot, you might accidentally go straight ahead to the auction galleries. NO. Turn left at the red door and you'll be rewarded with four large rooms of fabulous antiques, collectibles, costume and real jewelry, a bit of vintage clothing and just about everything else. Specialties include furniture, jewelry, vintage clothing, crystal, silver, pottery, linens, artwork, toys, decorative accessories, antiques, and much more!

There are more than 70 dealers and some of what they offer – the real stuff – is behind glass, but they'll quickly and cheerfully come and open it up for you. Many of the items in the open and closed booths also have sale signs, which is always a joy to see.

ANTIQUE MALL

CAROUSEL ANTIQUE CENTER

815 Lake Ave. / Lake Worth 33460 / (561) 533-0678
OPEN: Mon.-Fri. 10-5; Sat. 10-5:30; Sun. 1-5:30

This is a two-story 12,000-square-foot antique mall with many exhibitors and a wide variety of merchandise, from the very old to the ... well, not that new. It is an antique mall, after all, although there are plenty of collectibles around for those who like their "antiques" newer.

Carousel has been in business for 26 years – which tells you something about them – and they have about 75% vintage decorative and collectibles and 25% antiques. Many of the prices are excellent – particularly the 5 shelves in the upstairs section. That floor has a more open feeling than most antique malls, since it's not comprised of claustrophobic little stalls but is a wide open area where you can walk around and see – and touch – a lot of what's here. The jewelry and silver showcases in the front area are always a treat to look at.

I've always liked this place with its warm and cozy feeling, especially upstairs. The owner, Fred, works hard to keep his customers happy – and coming back. And they do.

CHARITY CONSIGNMENT
VALENTINA'S TREASURES

www.valentinastreasurespalmbeach.com
824 Lake Ave./ Lake worth 33460 / (561) 693-8636;
(800) 877-543-7770
OPEN: Mon.-Sun. 9-6 (but often closed).

The entrance is right off Lake Avenue, although the window on Lake filled with Marilyn Monroe memorabilia might give you a clue that it's not a Starbucks in there. Unfortunately, they're often closed. But if Valentina's Treasures is open, and you find it, you'll have a lot of fun, even though the prices are sometimes more likely to make you frown than smile. But it's a very large space, (3,000 square feet) and there's so much here, and a lot of it is well priced, so don't let a few outrageous tags scare you away from going through everything.

You'll find incredible things in the tightly packed rows and rows of vintage women's clothes. In the back they have vintage for men as well, specializing in original Versace men's shirts for $1,500, apparently quite a bargain. (Who knew?)

There's everything here from gorgeous costume jewelry to military caps to an old 1888 Regina music box with 20 metal disks, which they used before vinyl. For $1500, that seemed like a good deal, provided of course, you've always wanted a turn of the century "Victrola." And need one.

A few more things to know:

There's a parking lot in the back, on Dixie itself.

The photo on the Internet (see web page above) is exactly what it looks like – unlike many Internet photos of shops.

Next, they're right across from a great gym called The Zoo, in case you need help fitting into vintage gowns, which run smaller than modern garments.

WOMEN'S CLOTHING & ACCESSORIES (CONSIGNMENT)

FASHION EXCHANGE

702 Lake Ave. / Lake Worth 33460

(561) 547-9521

OPEN: Mon., Tues., Thurs. & Sat. 10-5; Wed. & Fri. 10-7; Sun. 12-5.

This women's and men's consignment shop is sometimes called "The Jewel of Lake Worth." But since it's slightly off the consignment circuit, not everyone knows about it. Which is a shame. Because this delightful shop, owned by Judy King since 1989, is well-stocked with designer-label clothes for men and women along with women's accessories at prices that are usually far lower than what you will find with similarly consigned clothes and accessories in nearby Palm Beach itself. How much lower? A Judith Leiber bag selling for $1,000 on the island was $400 here.

Fashion Exchange also has more hats than most resales, plus a few sections of good men's clothes, plus a few furs, and a large jewelry selection in a revolving display.

DON'T MISS: All the way in the back, behind the shoe section, you may find some more goodies.

FURNITURE, HOME DÉCOR & JEWELRY (CONSIGNMENT)

PALM BEACH HOME INTERIOR COLLECTION

www.palmbeachhome.com / Facebook: Palm Beach Home Interiors

716 Lake Ave. / Lake Worth 33469 / (561) 249-7002

OPEN: Mon.-Thurs. 10-5; Fri. Sat. 10-6; Sun. 12-5

This large emporium in Lake Worth seems to carry mostly "heavy" pieces like dining and bedroom sets. They also sell art, and up front, jewelry, both costume and real. If you're looking for attractive basic furniture, this is a good place to come. If you're looking for interesting accent pieces, the home décor is generally not as fetching as the furniture.

TIP: Hospice thrift shops often have good merchandise, especially TVs and furniture. Families often donate what's left of the deceased person's home or possessions to the hospice thrift shop, especially if they're grateful for the good final treatment received by their loved one. And, by the way, hospital thrift shops are always clean-looking.

WOMEN'S CLOTHES & ACCESSORIES (CONSIGNMENT)

SEQUELS BOUTIQUE

sequelsboutique.com
617 Lake Ave. / Lake Worth 33460 / (561) 586-0004
OPEN: Mon.-Fri. 11:30-5:30 Thurs.-Sat. 11:30-6:30;
Sun. 1-4

After the Happy Shopper's first quick trip here, her impression was sort of meh, OK. Nothing worth writing home or at least writing in this book about. There wasn't that much in it to go through which can be good and bad: good that there's room to walk around; bad that there isn't more to go through. (Yet)

Furthermore, Sequels is a combination of consignment (on the right side) and new, (on the left), and those kinds of places usually don't work very well.

But the second time, aha! The Happy Shopper spotted some nice consignment here and very little of it was over $20. Yes, occasionally you'll find something in the $30 range, like a Michael Kors dress, but that's still an incredible deal. And there was even a stunning turquoise new Badgley Mischka bathing suit priced at an unbelievable $18.

They carry a lot of Anthropologie and you'll find other labels like BCBG, Juicy Couture, Chico's, etc. Shoes were also pleasantly priced. As one example, a pair of Stuart Weitzman for $33.

There's also a selection of accessories such as handbags, jewelry, belt, scarves and a bit of jewelry, but nothing to write (home) about there.

So, this is a nice addition to the consignment/vintage shops of Lake Avenue, which include (from Dixie Highway down) VALENTINA'S, AFFLUENT FINDS, FASHION EXCHANGE and now this, in a different price range than the others. This place is not worth a separate trip yet, but don't skip it if you're wandering down Lake Avenue, which has increasingly become a great destination for consignment, vintage, art, crafts, and antique fans.

SHOP NEARBY: Next door at 615 Lake Avenue is LAKE WORTH JEWELERS, which sells much more than just jewelry. Ella Riggs, whom everyone in the neighborhood knows and likes, has stocked this shop with stunning Mary Frances handbags, outrageous hats, and truly outstanding costume and fine jewelry. If bling is your thing, this is the place to come to.

Lake Worth (Other)

(NOT TO SCALE)

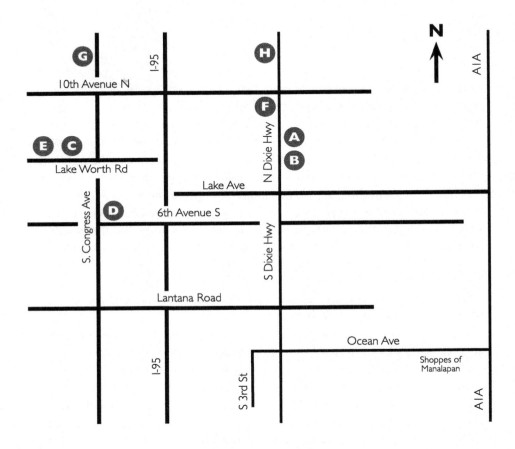

A .... All Good Things (p. 53)

B ..... Chase The Fox (p. 53)

C .... I Love Plus (p. 54)

D .... PBHC Thrift Store (p. 54)

E ..... Salvation Army Superstore (p. 55)

F ..... Sunrise Flea Market (p. 55)

G .... Vita Nova (p. 56)

H .... World Thrift (p. 56)

ANTIQUE MALL

ALL GOOD THINGS

328 N. Dixie Hwy. / Lake Worth 33460 (561)
547-7606

OPEN: Mon. 12-5:30; Tue.-Sat. 10:30-5:30; Sun. 12-5

This charming country-style antique mall is
much larger than it looks at first. That's because
the front rooms are just for starters, but keep
going, and you'll find not only more rooms but
an outdoor back annex – and something wonderful pops up at every turn –
which houses a small restaurant.

Most of this mall is indoors, but the front rooms are surprisingly sunny
for an antique mall. The brightness is one reason for the cheerful vibes at
All Good Things, as is the friendliness of the owner Doralea Asher and her
manager, Myrna Hammersley.

You get a good feeling at this 10-year-old mall. Many of the prices posted
by the 22 exhibitors are enticingly low to encourage turnover. "We turn and
burn," says the entrepreneurial Doralea. For example, a large mink stole in
good condition was a great catch at only $200 – and almost everything is
considerably less.

All Good Things is about half-and-half antique and collectibles, with
plenty of mostly-inexpensive vintage jewelry. You'll also find an entire section
of shabby-chic furniture – which they'll repaint for customers at a low price.
And don't forget to visit their large back section with vintage chairs, outdoor
furniture and garden accessories, which they'll proudly show you.

Something new is ALLEY CAT, which has two more rooms of antiques
and collectibles, representing 22 dealers. To enter, you go through All Good
Things.

FURNITURE & HOME DÉCOR (VINTAGE & CONSIGNMENT)

CHASE THE FOX

318 N. Dixie Hwy. / Lake Worth 33460 / (561) 494-5221
OPEN: Mon.-Wed. 10-7; Fri. Sat. 10-7

This thrift/vintage something-or-other is behind and slightly to the right of
ALL GOOD THINGS, so if you go first to the antique store (which you should)
you can't miss it – especially since the two-room barn-like building is bright
turquoise.

It calls itself a "consignment gallery" but it has the feel and look (but not the prices) that are more in line with a thrift shop. The two rooms contain furniture, antiques, knickknacks. If you make your way through this place, and ignore the tacky-looking furniture that's usually outside, you just may find something. But it's certainly not worth a separate trip; just a quick detour when you're in the "neighborhood."

WOMEN'S PLUS SIZE CLOTHING & ACCESSORIES (CONSIGNMENT)

I LOVE PLUS

www.iloveplus.com / Facebook: i love plus
3129 Lake Worth Rd. / Palm Springs 33461 /
(561) 642-1555
OPEN: Tues.-Sat. 10-5

I love "I Love Plus"–even though I don't fit in their clothes or their category. Despite their name and obvious focus on larger sizes – women from 18-32–those wearing smaller garments can also find some separates or even dresses that are just slightly larger. And their accessories, jewelry and handbags – which is the first thing I go for – can be worn by women of any size, not just what's called BBW (Big Beautiful Women).

Most of their merchandise is consigned, but a bit of the new is scattered around. Obviously enough women are looking for the beautiful larger merchandise that they mostly carry, and they're happy to come here and get it because they've been in business for over 15 years. Meanwhile, other plus-size consignment stores have all shrunk to nothing.

CLOTHES & MISCELLANEOUS (THRIFT)

PBHC THRIFT STORE

www.pbhab.com/main/thrift-store
Palm Beach Habilitation Center Campus /4522 S. Congress Ave.
Lake Worth 33461 / (561) 967-5993
OPEN: Mon.-Sat. 9-4

This large three-room thrift can be a bit hard to find, but the substantial boutique clothing section in the front makes it worth scouting out. In addition, there are often good finds in housewares and decorative accessories up front.

The second room behind it, the budget room, is typical low-priced thrift with everything reduced 50% if it's here a second month. The small back room has books, videos, and sometimes more unusual items. But it's the front room that is the "quality thrift."

Clothes & Miscellaneous (Thrift)

SALVATION ARMY SUPERSTORE
4001 Kirk Rd. / Lake Worth 33461 / (561) 642-1927
OPEN: Mon. -Fri. 9-5; Sat. 9-6.

The Salvation Army shops have been called "The Saks Fifth Avenue for the tightwad set." And there are plenty of bargains to be had–especially on Wacky Wednesdays when they give 50% off for seniors, teachers, and veterans. Nice. An especially good buy at many of their outlets is their selection of rock-bottom children's clothes. Whatever you buy, it'll be helping some organization that really needs the money.

NOTE: For more Salvation Army thrift stores in Southeast Florida, see p. 145.

Need category here

SUNRISE FLEA MARKET
1101-A N. Dixie Hwy. / Lake Worth 33460 / (561) 588 - 2898
OPEN: Mon.-Sat. 10-6; Sun. 10-5.

This was the best of the bunch with a promising future. It was really fun to go through the four rooms because there were some interesting things there. The clothes were stylish but not in good condition so forget that. But in the front rooms were also incredible deals on some good shoes ($2.99 a pair) and odd things someone might just want, like a real replica of the Taj Mahal or Korean plates. Well, someone might want them and there they are. That's what thrifting is all about. Discovering something you didn't know you wanted or needed.

In the back is a room with electronics and mostly men's clothes, and behind that some furniture that could make some home very happy, especially at that price.

VITA NOVA

3129 S. Congress Ave.
Palm Springs 33461 / (561) 434-2754
OPEN: Mon.-Sat. 9:30-6

When this attractive thrift shop first opened in Palm Springs (north of Lake Worth) it was so good you couldn't help but wonder whether they would be able to maintain the high level of merchandise and the low prices. One year later, through good donations, and excellent management, by Sandra R. Awong, and her assistant manager, Monica Grajales, they are still one of the better upscale resale shops.

Vita Nova is in its own building, and is just a medium-sized store, but it has a lot in it as well as going for it. They carry a small amount of new clothes, but most of it is gently worn, although the "new" is priced almost as low as the "resale." In addition to the apparel, they also stock some smart, new-looking furniture and artwork, as well as a large quantity of books. By the way, some employees speak Spanish.

WORLD THRIFT

2425 North Dixie Hwy. / Lake Worth 33460 / (561) 588-4050
OPEN: Mon.-Sat. 9-6. Cash only.

World Thrift is the shrine where all area thrifties (often secretly) come to worship. Many swear by (some at) this huge warehouse for orphaned clothes, some of which are practically given away at mind-boggling hard-to-believe prices.

Here's the good part. World Thrift is a clean, well-lit thrift shop with clothes neatly on the hangers. Cashiers move the lines quickly, except for Wednesdays, senior sale day. There's a tremendous turnover in merchandise, so even those who go a few times a week – and there are plenty of regulars – constantly find new bargains.

OK, now for the bad reports. It's so large, and clothes are divided according to type (say, blouses, short sleeves), and then color, but it's all mixed in. That means shoppers have to spend inordinate amounts of time going through everything if they're looking for a specific item in a certain color. This makes shopping hard work instead of play.

Some of the clothes have mild damage, or are missing buttons, or no size is listed, or something is slightly wrong with it so everything must be examined carefully. Smelled, also. Although they usually don't have that budget rock-bottom thrift shop turn-off smell when you enter, some of the clothes have a faint odor, especially after they've been in stock for a few days.

One more thing: the better handbags up front are sometimes fake, so you have to examine them carefully. (See p. 18 on how to tell if a handbag is real.)

NOTE: There are no dressing rooms, so wear a bathing suit or camisole underneath your clothes so you can try things on easily.

SALE INFORMATION: There's a big sign straight ahead as you walk in, plus another one in back of the row of cashiers telling you what color is either on sale or excluded from the sale that day. Wednesday is 50% off everything (for seniors 55+) except the newest merchandise.

THRIFT SHOPS NEARBY: ONE MORE TIME! THRIFT SHOP AND COFFEE BAR at 7600 South Dixie Hwy.(See p. 103) Also, it's not that near, but if you're looking for jeans and can't find one here – almost impossible with their huge selection – go to the GOODWILL at 3622 South Dixie Hwy. They have a large selection of mid-level jeans. "The very expensive ones go to the boutique shops, but we get them in the $60-$70 range," said one of the managers.

BARGAIN SAVING TIP: Thrift shops usually have the best bargains early in the week when they put most of their merchandise out. They also often have specific sales starting on Mondays, like shoes at 50% off. By Wednesday, or even Tuesday, the good ones may be gone.

Consignment shops are good to go to any time of the week, but generally, you'll find more on sale toward the end and beginning of the month. Many put clothes out at the beginning of each month and need to get rid of older merchandise first.

Lantana & Boynton Beach

(NOT TO SCALE)

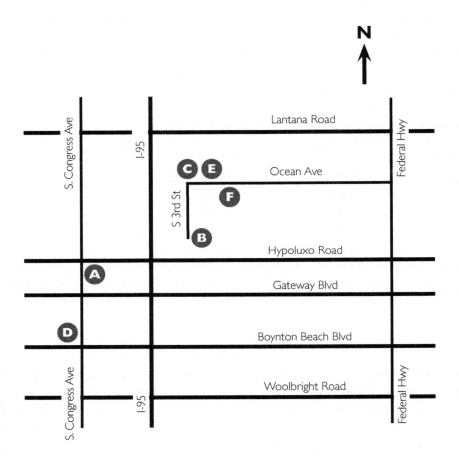

A .... Blessings and Bargains (p. 59)

B ..... Consignments by Sally (p. 59)

C .... Jamie's Classics (p. 60)

D .... Plato's Closet - Boynton Beach (p. 60)

E ..... Second Wind (p. 62)

F ..... Shades of Time (p. 62)

CLOTHES & MISCELLANEOUS (THRIFT)

BLESSINGS AND BARGAINS THRIFT STORE

Facebook: Blessings.Bargains
4755 N. Congress Ave. / Boynton Beach 33426 / (561) 296-9935
OPEN: Tues.-Sat. 10-5

The $1 rack outside with labels like Ann Taylor gives you an inkling of the bargains inside. There, you'll find long racks of thrifty clothes, clean but not very new looking. Still, there are better bargains, for example, a beautiful unworn beaded wedding gown with a matching purse and a long tulle train for $99 during a recent check.

Mostly, you encounter blouses for $2-$3, suits for $5, (men as well as women's– including a small section of men's plug sizes, something you don't see often), children's clothes and books, and golf clubs for $2 in this large clean shop that benefits Faith United Methodist Church in Boynton.

FURNITURE, HOME DÉCOR, JEWELRY & GIFTS (CONSIGNMENT)

CONSIGNMENTS BY SALLY

www.Consignmentsbysally.com
Lantana Center / 306 W. Mango St.
Lantana 33462 / (561) 547-4848
OPEN: Mon.-Sat. 10-5:30

Even if you're not in the market for stunning furniture, art deco, glassware, unique household accessories or charming and unusual gifts, you must come to Sally's to look at her collection. There's décor for every taste, and you might end up with something smashing for that lonely corner in your home that's begging to be filled.

Sally has been in the business for 17 years, and is very well liked, as is her shop. Everything in it looks new and beautiful. The 3,400-square-foot three-part store probably has more giftware, household accessories, and accent pieces – many a lot of fun – than other similar furniture consignments, maybe more than most new gift shops as well. Sally's also picks up and delivers.

HOW TO GET THERE: You may pass this mall without realizing what's here. Going south on Dixie, make a right on Ocean Avenue in Lantana, cross the railroad tracks, and then make an immediate left.

FURNITURE, HOME DÉCOR & JEWELRY (CONSIGNMENT)

JAMIE'S CLASSIC

www.jamiesclassics.com
223 E. Ocean Ave. / Lantana 33462
(561) 585-9808
OPEN: Mon.-Fri. 10-5:30; Sat. 10-5

Jamie is no longer owned by Jamie, but the name remains. The new owners have still filled it with contemporary furniture and smart home décor. The displays are almost all attractive (they have great couches, desks and dining tables) with many unusual one-of-a-kind objects. There's also a lot of original artwork, since many artists like to consign to this place. So you might come in looking for a chair, and end up falling in love with a painting that's perfect to take the place of one in your home that you never liked as well.

HOME ACCENT SHOP NEARBY: SECOND WIND (See p. 62)

RESALE CLOTHING – WOMEN AND MEN (TEENS)

PLATO'S CLOSET – BOYNTON BEACH

www.platosclosetboyntonbeach.com / Facebook: platos closet boynton beach
701 N. Congress Ave., Bay 3B / Boynton Beach 33426 / (561) 369-3550
OPEN: Mon.-Fri. 10-8; Sat. 10-6; Sun. 12-5

The emphasis here is on the mostly overlooked resale buying group: teens. All Plato's are stuffed with teen-oriented selections like Capris, tanks, sundresses, hoodies, black lights, lava lights, and that kind of thing. Looking through the racks, you'll spot many "younger" high-cred brands, like Aeropostal, Baby Phat, Bebe, Diesel, Ecko, Gap, Limited, Old Navy, and Rampage.

They claim to sell "fashion-savvy clothing for teens and young adults (men and women), promising "gently -used brand-name clothing and accessories" – shoes, purses, belts, jewelry – that have been purchased within the last year. Sizes for men and women go from extremely small to very large.

Bottom line: if you're over, say 21, or maybe even younger, you may not find clothes you're comfortable in. And you may feel that you're in the middle of a high school gab-fest when you come in. But if you're in the right age demographic, then you're going to find so much that's perfect for you, including lots of jeans.

It's all at a price less than what you'd pay in a store, but not ridiculously cheap unless it's on sale. Still, this teen-centric resale concept works so well that they have hundreds of franchises throughout the country.

NOTE: They don't consign clothes but buy them outright with immediate payment. But some have complained that you get so little for an item, you're almost better off donating them to a thrift shop and taking a deduction.

SALE INFORMATION: They have seasonal clearances announced at www. platoscloset.com. You can also join their e-mail club on line (www. platosclosetmiramar.com) and they'll send you a $5.00 coupon for your next visit! They promise no more than one e-mail a month afterwards. They'll also tell you of sales if you give them your e-mail address when you come in.

NOTE: Here are some additional Plato's Closets in Southeast Florida.

PLATO'S CLOSETS IN SOUTHEAST FLORIDA
(FRANCHISES AIMED AT TEENS)

Call first before making a special trip, because franchises often change.

BOCA RATON 2240 NW 19th St. / (561) 392-7075

BOYNTON BEACH 701 N. Congress Ave., Bay 3B / (561) 369-3550

CORAL SPRINGS 1259 N. University Dr. / (954) 575-2274

MIRAMAR 12176 Miramar Pkwy. / (954) 443-4414

MIAMI 13630 SW 120th St., #210 / (305) 259-2004

PALM BEACH GARDENS 11686 US Hwy. 1 / (561) 625-0059

PLANTATION 8120 W. Broward Blvd. / (954) 474-6944

WELLINGTON 10200 Forest Hill Blvd., Suite 110 / (561) 422-3838

WEST MIAMI 267 NW 82nd Ave. / (305) 2-PLATO'S

"The fashion magazines are suggesting that women wear clothes that are age appropriate. For me, that would be a shroud."

– Joan Rivers

HOME DÉCOR & SHABBY CHIC FURNITURE

SECOND WIND

Seondwindfl.com & facebook.com/secondwindfl
211 E. Ocean Ave. / Lantana 33462 / (561) 557-2188
OPEN: Tues.-Sat. 12-8.

This new shop is next to a juice/coffee/tea/smoothie bar called "Good Vibes," but that's what this place should be called because that's what it has: good vibes. Only some of what's here is consignment – the rest is purchased or made– but just about everything in this former private home is delightful.

Most of the repurposed home décor and shabby chic is made by the owner, Kathy Eberly, and the three rooms are full of whimsical, charming, beachy bistro gift items, funny wooden signs ("Give a Man an Inch and he Thinks he's a Ruler") and various coastal interiors. Prices start at $2 for adorable laminated book marks and there's more expensive beachy refurbished furniture in the small porch up front.

SHOP NEARBY: JAMIE'S CLASSIC (See p. 60)

SUNGLASSES (OUTLET)

SHADES OF TIME

www.shadesoftimeonline.com
214 E. Ocean Ave. / Lantana 33462 / (561) 540-8925
OPEN: Tues.-Sat. 9:30-5; Sun. Mon. 9:30-2:30

If you're in the market for reduced sunglasses, they sell thousands of them in this small shop, including major designers, all discounted with everything from $39-$500. The owner also has a once-a-year anniversary sale, usually Halloween weekend, when everything is 25%-60% off.

HOME DÉCOR SHOPS NEARBY: CONSIGNMENTS BY SALLY'S (See p. 59), JAMIE'S (See p. 60) & SECOND WIND (See p. 62)

*Marriage is a workshop where the husband
works and the woman shops.*

North Palm Beach & Lake Park

WOMEN'S & MEN'S CLOTHES, HOUSEWARES & FURNITURE (THRIFT)

ADOPT-A-CAT THRIFT
www.adoptacatfoundation.org / Facebook: AdoptACat
804 US Hwy. 1 / Lake Park 33403 / (561) 848-6930
OPEN: Mon.-Sat. 11-5; Sun. 11-3

A 25-pound cat welcomes you when you arrive, and the low prices are equally welcoming. This homey three-room shop sells everything at prices that are the cat's meow. The third furniture room is new and has a separate entrance and not worth visiting but thrifties will be pleased with the prices in the other two rooms. And what you buy helps spay and vaccinate homeless cats and have them placed for adoption. Anyone want a cute kitty?

WOMEN'S CLOTHING & ACCESSORIES (CONSIGNMENT)

CONSIGNED COUTURE
Facebook: Consigned Couture
932 Northlake Blvd. / North Palm Beach 33408
(561) 881-9005
OPEN: Mon.-Sat. 11-6

Looking for a handbag? Boy, have you come to the right place. Purses are propped, perched and hanging everywhere. Not to mention dangling from a beam on the ceiling, leaning against the walls, and sitting patiently in back of the counter. And in the glass showcase is an especially attractive selection of jewelry. You have definitely arrived at accessory heaven.

The clothes in Elizabeth Araujo's crowded shop are great, too, making browsing a wonderful adventure. So don't miss a trip to this well-stocked consignment store on Northlake Boulevard that's overflowing with desirable and often high-end items, mostly for women. Some is even geared toward a younger crowd.

CONSIGNMENT SHOP NEARBY: LADIES CHOICE (See p. 87)

If men liked shopping, they'd call it research.

DECORATORS RESOURCE

www.decoratorsresource.net
333 US Hwy. I / Lake Park 33403 / (561) 845-9648
OPEN: Mon. – Sat. 9:30-5:30; Sun. 12: -5

If you're decorating a home – or you're a designer or dealer – you should know about this humongous (10,000 square feet) high-end furniture store. But if you're looking for bargains, the only way you might find one here is if you go to their website, and on the upper right hand corner of the front page, sign up for their special discounts.

But if you don't mind spending more to get more, then this place has it all, from kitchen, patio, garden, and barware accessories to dining, seating and garden furniture, lighting and home décor items. They've been around for 15 years, always a good sign.

DEJA NEW GALLERY

www.facebook.com/DejaNewGallery
212 US Hwy. I / North Palm Beach 33408 /(561) 844-1151
OPEN: 11- 4

It's a furniture store and art gallery, carrying everything from lighting fixtures to …. a butter churn...to a piano that one can play – for $250. (At that low price, how well it plays depends on how well you play.) The inventory is kept fresh; the prices are fair.

ST. MARK'S THRIFT SHOP

208 US Hwy. I / Lake Park 33403 / (561) 863-8516
OPEN: Wed.-Sat. 10-4

You'll find three large rooms here: one for furniture, chandeliers, lamps, an occasional piano, electronics and books. The second room is glassware, kitchenware, children's clothes, CDs and movies. The third room has a boutique rack with name brands, a jeans rack, miscellaneous clothes (including men's), purses, pictures, and shoes. Lots and lots of shoes.

Another nice thing: no tax because it's affiliated with a church.

HIGH-END FURNITURE & HOME DÉCOR (CONSIGNMENT)

TRUE TREASURES CRYSTAL TREE PLAZA

www.truetreasuresinc.com / Facebook: True Treasures Antiques Fine Consignments

1201 US Hwy., Suite 15 / North Palm Beach 33408 / (561) 625-9569

OPEN: Mon-Sat. 10-6; Sun. 12-5.

The most upscale of the two True Treasures, this one is for the connoisseur who likes to browse where great art, Persian rugs, fine china, unusual antiques mingle with contemporary furniture. A polite way of saying that this is the more expensive of the two.

CLOTHES, HOME DÉCOR & MISCELLANEOUS (CONSIGNMENT)

VAL'S RED HAT

Facebook: Vals red hat Consignment Shop

1183 Old Dixie Hwy. / Lake Park 33403

(561) 568-8257

OPEN: Mon.-Fri 10-5; Sat. 10-whenever

Are you in for a surprise when you enter this place! It looks like an optical shop with two large iconic Shepherd's glasses. But inside... wow. Five thousand square feet of everything you could possibly want and so much is unique and delightful. You probably won't buy the real musk that was there for $2,500, but you will probably buy so much that's there for a lot lot less. And what fun it is to walk from room to room, alcove to alcove. And if you don't find what you're looking for, ask Val, because she keeps even more unusual fare in their storage units.

Yes, there's some clothes, like a large alcove just of "After 5's." but there's so much than what you at first think. Even the owner, Val, is more than a shop owner: she's a licensed optician, a licensed massage therapist, and a licensed real estate broker. "This is another hat I wear," she says of this shop that attracts people from Singer Island, Ibis and North Palm Beach

NORTHWOOD – A MINI ANTIQUE ROW

Whether you call it "North South Beach" or "Mini Antique Row," this charming three-block area in West Palm Beach is sprinkled with a collection of unusual shops, artsy windows, antiques, collectibles and at last count – things change here a lot – 22 restaurants, four bakeries, a coffee house, and more.

What you'll find in Northwood usually costs far less than at most antique shops elsewhere. Indeed, some of these stores were originally located on Dixie's more expensive Antique Row before settling here.

You'll find this section north of downtown West Palm Beach, but don't go far past the shopping area. It borders Riviera Beach. Enough said. But you'll be perfectly safe (and happy!) wandering down this European-style street.

The atmosphere is casual – the owner of one gallery came out to greet a customer barefoot– and the last Friday of every month, from 6-9 PM, they have an "Art and Wine Promenade" with wine tastings, street-side artists, and live entertainment.

Here, alphabetically, are the top antique, vintage and consignment shops in Northwood.

AAA FURNITURE
412, 414, & 416 Northwood Rd. / (561) 833-9921
OPEN: Mon.-Fri. 11-5; Sat. 10-3

"A little bit of everything" is how they describe the three rooms they've kept full for 30 years. The 3,300 square feet consists of the contents of homes (they buy entire estates) with surprisingly low prices, and there's enough room for larger pieces, such as couches, dining tables, etc. But not enough room to easily get around!

The only thing that separates us from the animals is our ability to accessorize.

CIRCA WHO

www.circawho.com
531 Northwood Rd. / (561) 655-5224
OPEN: Tues. Wed. Thurs. 11-4 and other non-set times.

Owner Tracy DeRamus has filled this bright almost new-looking shop with mostly 20th Century "vintage Palm Beach, type furniture," she said. The 2,400-square-feet two-room antique shop stands out amidst the others by having some better pieces in practically pristine condition, such as the pagoda mirror, zebra vase, and driftwood table at $1600, 2400 and $350 respectively. In other words, no bargains, but lots of very good objects.

DIANE'S BOUTIQUE

515 ½ Northwood Rd. / (561) / 317- 6091
OPEN: who knows?

Don't ask owner Diane McKinnie when her consignment clothes & accessories shop is open because she doesn't know, so you certainly won't either. Inside are three rows of shoes, handbags, and separates, and even some Lilly Pulitzer's up front. Alas, the prices are often harder to find than the hours. and there's so much stuff in this small shop it's hard to get around.

LEFT HAND LOUIE

525 Northwood Rd. / (561) 835-2121
OPEN: most days 11am-5 pm.

Emilie Marie has always carried beautiful jewelry that people come from all over the world to buy—including well-dressed celebrities like Sally Ann Howes, who have been photographed wearing one of Emilie's pieces. "Palm Beach Society" magazine described her jewelry as "affordable, stylish, unusual…arty." Her Facebook page (https://www.facebook.com/LeftHandLouis) gives you an idea of the type of jewelry you'll find there. She moves around, so call before you go.

LOLA'S MAGIC CLOSET

515 Northwood Rd. / (561) 543-9776
OPEN: Mon.-Sat 10-4

This four-year-old shop didn't look very magical or for that matter, inviting-looking, but it's all vintage, which often has that look.

MY NEW OLD CHAIR INC.

431 Northwood Rd. / (561) 833 -0430

OPEN: Mon.-Fri. 9-5

Basically, this is an upholstery and home décor shop, but they also sell some old pieces that they've reupholstered and refinished. And some unfinished ones too, at much lower prices

NANCY'S VINTAGE WAREHOUSE

nancysvintagewarehouse.com

980 Service St., Unit 22 / West Palm Beach 33407/ (561) 308-2220

OPEN: By appointment.

Nancy's is a few blocks west of Northwood Village, but this place is worth the detour not only because everyone likes Nancy, but also because she often has warehouse sales. She also regularly carries an impressive collection of vintage Lilly Pulitzers, art, furniture and jewelry, not to mention that she has Annie Sloan Chalk paint workshops. Call before going.

NORTHWOOD ANTIQUES

420 Northwood Rd. /(561) 588-0129

OPEN: Mon.-Sat. 10-5. Also open some evenings.

Antiques, estates, rugs, palm trees, old trains, and two large white Foo dogs outside welcome you to what's there.

NORTHWOOD GLASS ART AND GIFTS

Northwoodglasart.com

524 Northwood Rd. / (561) 329-4280

OPEN: Tues.-Sat. 10:30-5

This has always been one of the loveliest shops on the street, filled with beautiful glass jewelry, bracelets, frames, plates, memory boxes, and more. They also have a small amount of consigned jewelry and woodworking pieces, plus classes, a lovely ambience, and a nice owner.

PURPLE BOUGAN-VILLA

423 Northwood Rd. / (561) 246-1777

OPEN: Tues.-Sat. 12-5

They're chock full of unusual vintage and antique furnishings, home décor & gifts, and what they describe as "eclectic and fun."

SOMETHING LIVELY

Sometinglively.com
540 Northwood Rd. /(561) 319-3151
OPEN: Mon. 10-3; Tues.-Sat. 10-5

Not only will you find something lively, but something different here as well. For example, a 10'x10' bar that came from the La Gorse Country Club – where Al Capone was once a partner – was available. (For only $25,000.)

Then, there was the swan dining table… well, there are lots here, and David does a lot too, from having regular auctions to planning a new mall. In the meantime, he has free wine tastings the first Friday of each month, (6-9 pm) and the 2nd Saturday, an art walk through the gallery, also 6-9 PM. Stay tuned: he's always doing something interesting. And something lively.

STAMBO'S

511 Northwood Rd. / (561) 328-7613
HOURS: variable

Describing themselves as "where there's something for everyone," they're especially heavy on nice consigned clothes, including jewelry, sunglasses, shoes, jeans, separates for men and women and more.

In addition to racks of clothes, they carry home décor, collectibles, furniture, lamps, art, vintage, antique, modern, not to mention various knickknacks, comic books, Persian rugs and whatever happens to come in at that time. Check it out– if they're open.

"A bargain is something you can't use at a price you can't resist."

– Franklin P. Jones

Palm Beach

(NOT TO SCALE)

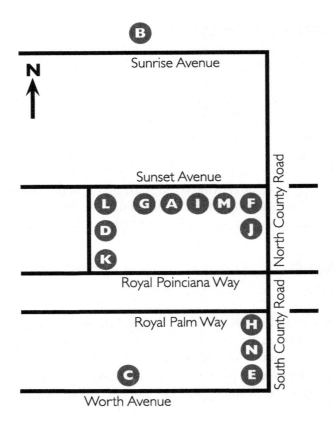

A.... Attitudes Consignment (p. 72)

B..... Avenue Revue (p. 72)

C.... Balatro (p. 73)

D.... Cassie and James Boutique (p. 74)

E..... Church Mouse (p. 75)

F..... Classic Collections (p. 76)

G.... Déjà Vu (p. 77)

H.... Fashionista (p. 79)

I....... Goodwill Embassy Boutique (p. 79)

J....... Groovy Palm Beach Vintage (p. 80)

K.... Maxim's of Paris (p. 81)

L..... Paradise Lost (p. 82)

M.... Razamataz Consignment Boutique (p. 83)

N.... Sequin (p. 83)

SPECIAL SHOPPING TOUR OF PALM BEACH – ONE BLOCK OF UPSCALE CONSIGNMENT SHOPS

The eastern end of Sunset Avenue/North County Road in Palm Beach with seven shops all clustered together is the Holy Grail for resale shoppers. The stores start at the end of North County Road, then circle around to Sunset Avenue. Start at:

GROOVY PALM BEACH at 108 N. County Road, a vintage shop for men and women. (See p. 80.)

CLASSIC COLLECTIONS at 118 N. County Road, is a pricey women's consignment shop. (See p. 76.)

Then circle around to Sunset and go to:

ATTITUDES at 212 Sunset, a woman's consignment shop (See p. 72.)

EMBASSY BOUTIQUE (a classy **GOODWILL**) at 210 Sunset. (See p. 79.)

RAZAMATAZ a posh women's consignment shop at 208 Sunset. (See p. 83.)

DÉJÀ VU at 219 Royal Poinciana Way (it actually fronts on Sunset between Attitudes and Paradise Lost), is a very high-end women's consignment shop. (See p. 77.)

PARADISE LOST for gifts and home décor is at 210 Sunset, (also 219 Royal Poinciana Way #3) across from Deja Vu. (See p. 82.)

Then, walk down the via between Deja Vu and Paradise Lost to:

CASSIE & JAMES BOUTIQUE, a consignment shop for children and adults at 219 Royal Poinciana Way #2 (also 2 Via Testa). (See p. 74.)

Continue toward Royal Poinciana and there's the new **MAXIM'S OF PARIS** at 219 Royal Poinciana Way, Via Testa #4. (See p. 81.)

Finally, one block north of Sunset at 227 Sunrise Ave., is **AVENUE REVUE**, another upscale women's consignment shop, this one only open in the morning. (See p. 72.)

FOR A SECOND PALM BEACH SHOPPING TOUR, SEE P. 75.

FOR MORE SHOPS IN PALM BEACH, SEE BELOW.

WOMEN'S CLOTHING & ACCESSORIES (CONSIGNMENT)

ATTITUDES CONSIGNMENT BOUTIQUE

www.attitudesofpalmbeach.com
212 Sunset Ave. / Palm Beach 33480
(561) 832-1666
OPEN: Mon.-Sat. 10-5

Attitudes is the largest of the Sunset consignment/vintage shops, and is often a little less expensive than the others. Occasionally, here you'll even spot a lovely sight to behold: a brand new garment with the tag still dangling from it.

For those looking to splurge, there are designer heavyweights like St. Johns and Chanels sprinkled in among their clothes and handbags. They're about one-third the regular price. The St. Johns rack is on the left-hand side in the back. Chanel and better bags are to the right in the glass showcase as soon as you enter.

You'll also find some affordable footwear here, often even Stubbs & Wootton shoes, worn by the Palm Beach fashion cognoscenti. Among other unique items: sometimes you'll see equestrian pants, plus ski and winter jackets for the snowbirds.

NOTE: Parking on Sunset is for one hour only and is strictly enforced. If you get carried away and forget to move your car, what you bring home from your shopping expedition may be a parking ticket.

WOMEN'S CLOTHING & ACCESSORIES (CONSIGNMENT)

AVENUE REVUE

227 Sunrise Ave. / Palm Beach 33480 / (561) 655-3235
OPEN: Mon.-Sun. 7 AM–1 PM; appointments after 1

Avenue Revue is unique. Yes, they have the high-end designer women's apparel and accessories – including jewelry and furs – that you'd expect in Palm Beach. But the owner, Peggy Sue Middleton, is a ballroom dancer, and sells competition ballroom gowns of the kind you see on "Dancing with the Stars."

This very small but well-stocked consignment shop – the sole one that is open only in the mornings – has top quality garments every place you turn. They also carry "spectacular gowns for the Palm Beach balls, and for the mother-of-the-bride occasions," says the owner. Plus a rack of what she calls "Worth Avenue labels" at good prices.

Ms. Middleton is also a personal shopper for a select clientele, and that, along with her being a ballroom dancer, would make you expect to see her all dolled up when you come here. But as she puts it: "I don't want to look better than my clients."

SHOPS NEARBY: Sunset Avenue with all the consignment shops is a block away. PALM BEACH BICYCLE TRAIL SHOP, which rents bikes, in-line skates, and mopeds, is right next door at 223 Sunrise Ave.

WOMEN'S CLOTHING (VINTAGE)

BALATRO

408 Hibiscus / Palm Beach 33480 / (561) 832-1817
OPEN: Mon.-Sat. 10-6 or by appointment.

Behind Chanel, and next to the new John Barrett Salon at Bergdorf Goodman, (straight from New York) is this high-end women's (and occasional men's) vintage clothing emporium. What type of vintage? Top of the line, that's for sure. "If I find something good enough I'll put it in here," says the owner, Tiffany Freisberg, who, with her mother, hand chooses every thing that ends up in this unique shop.

"We don't take consignment," she explained. Instead, they carefully select the items themselves, specializing in vintage Chanel & Dior—mostly French and a few English high-end designers. That includes an impressive selection of vintage jewelry – a lot of Miriam Haskell and Chanel – along with the more predominant separates, gowns and even costumes.

Originally an art gallery, a few paintings remain here, but most of them– along with chairs, antiques, objets d'art and more– have moved to another BALATRO at 3508 S. Dixie. Fortunately, the clothing-related items remained and are featured here, providing a welcome addition to the high-end consignments of modern clothes in Palm Beach.

WOMEN'S & CHILDREN'S CLOTHING & ACCESSORIES (CONSIGNMENT)

CASSIE AND JAMES BOUTIQUE

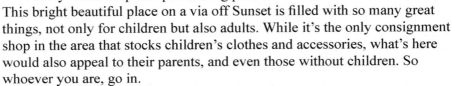

Facebook: Cassie and James Boutique
219 Royal Poinciana Way, #2 (or 2 Via Testa) /
Palm Beach 33480
(561) 366-8466
OPEN: Tues.-Sat. 10:30-5

A very small shop that packs a big punch. This bright beautiful place on a via off Sunset is filled with so many great things, not only for children but also adults. While it's the only consignment shop in the area that stocks children's clothes and accessories, what's here would also appeal to their parents, and even those without children. So whoever you are, go in.

Unfortunately, it's easy to miss Cassie and James Boutique since it doesn't front the Sunset "strip." But just look for DEJA VU and the new PARADISE LOST on Sunset and walk up that via and you can't miss it.

The friendly owner, Susan, uses Facebook to announce sales and new items that have come in. So join the Facebook Page for additional Sale and Discount information: Cassie and James Boutique.

CONSIGNMENT SHOP NEARBY: This is just a few steps down the via from the new PARADISE LOST. (See p. 82)

ESTATE SALES:

If you're looking for estate sales, or you just like to traipse around lovely gardens in beautiful homes looking at nice things, then go to the Palm Beach Daily News classified ads for "estate" or "garage sales" listings, generally held on the upcoming weekend.

The owners, trying to dispose of their fancy household goods, place many of the ads. But some people, like, Lou Ann Wilson-Swan, puts these sales together. And she'll place you on her popular mailing list ("Lulu's Stuff") of upcoming estates sales if you call her at (561) 655-1529.

SECOND PALM BEACH SHOPPING TOUR – THRIFT, CLOTHING CONSIGNMENT & JEWELRY OUTLET

There's also a second lesser-known Mecca for resale and outlet lovers, near Worth Avenue and a few minutes away from the N. County/Sunset Consignment shops (See p.).

Start at: **CHURCH MOUSE**, a high-end thrift shop at 378 S. County Road. (See p. 75)

SEQUIN OF PALM BEACH, a jewelry outlet, is slightly north at 330 S. County Road. (See p. 83)

FASHIONISTA, a very pricey women's consignment shop is at 298 S. County Road. (See p. 79)

FOR ANOTHER SHOPPING TOUR OF PALM BEACH CONSIGNMENTS, SEE P. 71.

CLOTHES, FURNITURE & MISCELLANEOUS (QUALITY THRIFT)

CHURCH MOUSE

www.bbts.org/churchmouse
Facebook: pbchurchmouse
378 S. County Rd. / Palm Beach 33480
(561) 659-2154
OPEN: Mon.-Sat. 10-4

This shop is indisputably the best thrift in all of Palm Beach County, perhaps any place in the world for high-end clothes at low-end prices. Not to mention all kinds of other wonderful miscellaneous home and personal products that are all around.

This bustling eight-room shop is filled with what used to be in some of the finest Palm Beach homes (and closets), now at prices that are amazing for what you get. Especially the women's evening gowns, immediately to the right when you enter. They also have a large alcove for men's clothes in the back to the right, all like new and many with expensive labels. Elsewhere you'll find good jackets, shoes, books, magazines, children's clothes and toys, DVDs, home and kitchen do-dads, pillows, small appliances, glassware, and whatever else they acquire from local homes.

DON'T MISS: It's easy to miss the sale explanation. Upon entering the main door, immediately look at the wall across you for the colored-ticket rotation code.

NOTE: Closes in June; reopens in October. (The June closing always has a special sale.)

JEWELRY OUTLET SHOP NEARBY: SEQUIN. (See p. 83)

WOMEN'S CLOTHING & ACCESSORIES (CONSIGNMENT & NEW)

CLASSIC COLLECTIONS – PALM BEACH

www.classiccollectionsofpalmbeach.com
Facebook: Classic Collections of Palm Beach
118 N. County Rd. / Palm Beach 33480
(561) 833-3633
OPEN: Mon.-Sat. 10-5:30

This designer and high-fashion resale boutique has some new clothes mingled in with the rest. Everything is beautiful, but most of it very pricey – like the rack of St. Johns and Chanels to the left when you enter – although it's way under the original cost, which is often quite ridiculous anyway.

Yes, they do have Judith Leiber bags and Chanel quilted purses for $1,000+ each. But they've also carried a Kate Spade shoulder bag for $50 and a Pucci purse for $190. There's usually a rack or two in the back section where you may find some markdowns. But it'll still probably be pretty pricey. Occasionally, there are a few furs, but accessories are their strong point. Under glass, you can find some original as well as consigned costume jewelry.

A real find, though, are the luxury shoes up front, like Chanel, Manolo Blahnik, Jimmy Choo, Gucci, Prada, Yves St. Laurent, and other big names marked down. So kick up your heels and buy some new ones while you're at it.

SHOP NEARBY: This is very near EVELYN & ARTHUR Palm Beach at 100 N. County Road.

"I base most of my fashion sense on what doesn't itch."

– Gilda Radner

FIVE SPECIAL SALES IN PALM BEACH THAT YOU DON'T WANT TO MISS

1) CHURCH MOUSE CLOSING SALE: Generally early in June, the best thrift shop in all of Palm Beach County, the Church Mouse at 378 S. County Road (see p. 75) closes for the summer. The week before, everything goes on sale and is progressively reduced all week.

2) POSH SALE: Around mid-February, this annual sale is held, and socialites and celebrities like Arlene Dahl donate their gently-used clothes for this "fashionable philanthropy" event that helps the Lighthouse International's services for the blind. www.poshsale.org gives the dates of the sale.

3) ST. EDWARD'S CHURCH: This indoor/outdoor sale is held around Easter at the St. Edward's Catholic Church at 144 N. County Road.

4) STUBBS & WOOTTON at 4 Via Parigi: The Palm Beach "foot look" is either Gucci loafers without socks or Stubbs & Wootton slipper-like shoes with distinctive logo. The shoes regularly cost close to $400 each. But on the Monday after Easter, for one week, they're 50% off.

5) C.ORRICO at 336 S. County Road has had an annual Memorial Day Weekend sale for over 20 years. But they always have a great sale going on in their back rooms.

WOMEN'S CLOTHING & ACCESSORIES (CONSIGNMENT)

DÉJÀ VU
219 Royal Poinciana Way #5 (212 Sunset)
Palm Beach 33480 / (561) 833-6624
OPEN: Mon.-Sat. 10-5:30

For almost a quarter of a century, Déjà Vu has carried top quality (and expensive) consigned women's clothes. Indeed, they have the largest selection of discounted Chanel outside of a regular full-price Chanel shop.

Like the other upscale resales on this street, nothing looks like anybody ever wore it. Which could be true, since many of the well-heeled (sometimes literally) locals who consign to Déjà Vu have very large closets in their huge homes and may not even know what's in them. Or perhaps they've worn something once to a Palm Beach party or gala, and don't dare wear it again to another one for fear that people will talk. And some will!

Not surprisingly in Florida, some of the furs are new. (Even when it doesn't get that cold in Florida, there are women who sometimes wear their furs.) Plus, they carry expensive accessories, such as Chanel and Judith Leiber, at a little less than at standard stores. Still, if you haven't fainted from the prices, walk on to the smaller third room in back and the tiny alcove off of it. There are some handbags right before that back room which is easy to miss. Also, some of blouses higher up immediately to your right in the back room sometimes have additional reductions.

DON'T MISS: Colored-ticket rotation may not be noticed, since the first sign is only posted in the second room, high up to the left.

SALE INFORMATION: In August, they have 50% off everything except Chanel.

NOTE: The only try-on room is a communal one, so wear your best underwear.

HOW JACKIE KENNEDY ONASSIS MADE CONSIGNMENT SHOPS POPULAR

It wasn't always as acceptable as it is now to go to thrift and consignment stores. In the early '70's, there were only a few consignment shops, and going to a thrift store meant you couldn't afford to shop in a retail store.

But in the 70's, word got out that Jackie Onassis was secretly selling her new clothes to Encore, a consignment shop in Manhattan that was established in 1954. It seems that Jackie's super-rich husband, Aristotle Onassis, had put her on a "strict" clothing allowance of $25,000 a month. She converted this to cash by buying expensive new clothes, and then secretly selling them to Encore.

Word leaked out, women went to Encore to buy her clothes, and suddenly, it became fashionable to shop at consignments. Today, thanks to Jackie, that area of resale stores remains extremely popular. (See p. 45)

"I buy expensive suits. They just look cheap on me."
– Warren Buffet

FASHIONISTA

http://fashionistapalmbeach.tumblr.com / Facebook: Fashionista Palm Beach
298 S. County Rd. / Palm Beach 33480 / (561) 249-6302
OPEN: Tues.-Sat. 10–6

    This shop is so exclusive that there's no way to know from the name, door or window that it's resale. They're so discreet they're not even with the other consignments on Sunset/North County Road, although a few of their customers seeking not only luxury but real bargains, sneak a couple of blocks south to go to the Church Mouse, the famous upscale thrift shop. Fashionista, though, is definitely one of the most upscale (expensive) consignment shops in three counties, with plenty of merchandise to choose from. If luxury is your game, and money not a consideration, this is your place.

EMBASSY BOUTIQUE GULFSTREAM GOODWILL

210 Sunset Avenue / Palm Beach 33480
(561) 832-8199
OPEN: Mon.-Sat. 9-5; Sun. 10-5

    Goodwill pulls out some of the highest quality donations they receive and places them in this three-room store. In fact, you occasionally see some of the same names as in the nearby upscale consignments. Some of the owners of consignment shops on this street donate their unsold goods and garments to Goodwill if they don't move in their own places.

    Naturally, the clothes are not as deftly displayed, and they're not usually in as pristine condition. But even superb condition Brooks Brothers tuxes have been just one of the finds among the very large selection of men's clothes. But mostly, they have an abundance of women's clothes, ranging from casual to couture, from low price to not-so-high price.

    If you're looking for bargains on better women's clothes, to the right in the front room are three open "closets," often carrying Lilly Pulitzer, St. John, Armani etc. It's also fun to rummage through the bins and boxes to the right of the entrance, which are filled mostly with lesser-priced handbags. Jewelry is under glass to the left, but the best pieces are displayed in the upright closed showcase to the left in back of the first section. Especially attractive clothes or higher-end handbags may be hanging in back of the register.

You have to look carefully in the second and third rooms (and the alcove in-between) because there's a lot stuffed in here. Some shoes, for example, are almost hidden above and below the clothes in the third room.

DON'T MISS: The windows up front are very small and you can only see the merchandise from the outside. Some of it is very good, so stop and look before you enter.

NOTE: The price tags attached to all garments have a colored string, the color on sale that day. The signs explaining the color code are usually in front of the register.

SALE INFORMATION: Wednesday is Senior Day with 25% off everything

SHOPS NEARBY: Nothing as inexpensive.

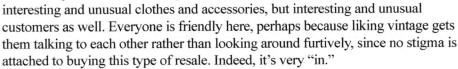

MEN'S & WOMEN'S VINTAGE CLOTHES & ACCESSORIES

GROOVY PALM BEACH VINTAGE

Facebook: Groovy Palm Beach Vintage
108 N. County Rd. / Palm Beach 33480
(561) 628-9404
OPEN: Mon.-Sat. 11-5 in season;
by appointment off season

Groovy Palm Beach Vintage not only has interesting and unusual clothes and accessories, but interesting and unusual customers as well. Everyone is friendly here, perhaps because liking vintage gets them talking to each other rather than looking around furtively, since no stigma is attached to buying this type of resale. Indeed, it's very "in."

As the name suggests, Groovy specializes in the colorful Carnaby Street psychedelic garments from the 60's-80's. The owner, Mr. Fredricks, is an expert on clothes of this era, and he carries items you won't find in any other vintage shops. There's also an extensive collection of Emilio Pucci designed in his lifetime, along with Lilly Pulitzer of the 60's and 70's, some with the original labels. (They have the largest selection of vintage Pucci and Lilly Pulitzer anyplace.)

About one-quarter of the clothes are men's, and the rest are women's. You'll also find knickknacks and vintage accessories, including some unique and well-priced jewelry in showcases throughout the store.

DON'T MISS: This place itself could be missed – but don't. The window on the street is very small; the shop is on North County between Royal Poinciana Way and Sunset.

80

WOMEN'S CLOTHES (CONSIGNMENT)

MAXIM'S OF PALM BEACH

219 Royal Poinciana Way, Via Testa #4 / Palm Beach 33480
OPEN: Mon.-Sat. 9:30-6; Sun. 12 to 5.

Just what we needed: a wonderful new upscale women's consignment shop in Palm Beach. Indeed, as soon as you enter Maxim's designer boutique, with the chandeliers – reflecting off mirrored walls illuminating the French lilac interiors – you feel the elegance and glamour of old Palm Beach. One of only two shops sharing the Courtyard on Via Testa, they're managed by staff with over 50 years combined experience in haute fashion, poised to assist you in choosing just the right look.

And what a roster to choose from! You'll immediately find yourself amidst names such as Hermes, Louboutin, Chanel, Pucci, Akris, Fendi, Choo, Cartier, Valentino, Oscar, Louis Vuitton, Gucci, Armani, Cavalli, Dolce & Gabbana, YSL, Christian Dior and many more. The knowledgeable sales staff at Maxim's will help you achieve the perfect look for any occasion - from classic casual to daytime chic to the most elegant evening ensemble.

Accessories anyone? Whether its an ultra-smart Bottega handbag for your next luncheon, a pair of Prada pumps and a Christopher Ross belt for the board meeting, a Suzanne Hat and Ray-Bans for sailing, or bejeweled Judith Leiber earrings for your next charity event - this exciting new addition to the Palm Beach consignment world will feature the most desirable names in shoes, bags, scarves, belts, hats and jewelry on the Island.

NOTE: Testa's Restaurant, Palm Beach's oldest eatery, will give you a 15% discount on same-day, non-sale purchases at Maxim's. (And go for Testa's renowned coconut cake.) You can easily find parking on Royal Poinciana Way, and if you park on the far side of the street, across from the grass divider, you get two hours instead of the one they give you directly across from the restaurants.

The only man who really needs a tail coat is a man with a hole in his trousers.

—John Taylor

PARADISE LOST

www.ParadiseLostPalmBeach.com
219 Royal Poinciana Way, Via Testa #3 (or 214 Sunset Ave) / Palm Beach 33480
(561) 223-2284
OPEN in Season: Mon-Sat 9:30-7; Sun. 12-6.
Off Season: Mon.-Sat. 10:30-6; Sun. 12:30-5

Paradise Lost, the aptly named anchor shop on the renowned Via Testa, is a must- see when visiting Palm Beach's famous Sunset Avenue consignment district. The shop – well known to the international set (from Tanya Pierce days) for fascinating gifts, objets d' art and home décor - has expanded into the only true emporium on Palm Beach Island.

In addition to Herend, Lalique and Waterford; English, French and German china; and antiques, oils and sculptures, there are now full men's and women's departments featuring designer shoes, clothing and accessories, including bags, fine and costume jewelry and luggage, much of it from homes on the island.

There is no other consignment shop in Palm Beach where one can find, for instance, that definitive Cartier bracelet or Chanel handbag for her, as well as that au courant Hermes necktie or pair of Ferragamo loafers for him. And at the same time, purchase a couple of polo mallets, a 17th century French painting, or a mounted John Sutton Kerr safari head. The variety is incredible.

One may spend several hours in Paradise Lost and not see quite everything, so one should leave time enough to shop among familiar names: Louboutin, Prada, Dresden, Gucci, Coach, Royal Copenhagen, Belleek, Versace, Royal Crown Derby, Judith Leiber, Miriam Haskell, Zegna, Vuitton, Brioni, Tod's, etc. And the endearing staff at Paradise Lost caters to every need—all of us especially like Sean –helping each visitor to leave completely satisfied and utterly delighted at the experience. Tell them Paulette sent you and they may give you a discount.

NEARBY SHOP: The new MAXIM'S OF PALM BEACH (See p. 81) is just a few shops down in the Via Testa Courtyard.

*No one in the world needs a mink coat
but a mink.*

– Murray Banks

WOMEN'S CLOTHING & ACCESSORIES (CONSIGNMENT)

RAZAMATAZ
CONSIGNMENT BOUTIQUE

208 Sunset Ave. / Palm Beach 33480
(561) 655-2135
OPEN: Mon.-Sat. 10-5

The larger of the two Razamataz stores, this one offers more clothes and accessories than its Boca sister (See p. 20) This 20-year-old small but beautiful consignment boutique is easily laid out. And even though there's plenty to please, you don't feel crowded.

Mostly, you'll find upscale designer blouses, slacks, skirts, evening gowns, sunglasses, handbags and jewelry here. They sometimes carry furs, and while they'll warm you up, they may put a chill in your bank account. Occasionally, they have sales in a hidden room in the back (ask).

JEWELRY (OUTLET)

SEQUIN PALM BEACH

Facebook: sequin.palmbeach
330 S. County Rd. / Palm Beach 33480 / (561) 833-7300
OPEN Mon.-Sat. 10-6; Sun. 11-6.

For twenty years they only sold their line of popular line of costume jewelry bracelets, earrings, necklaces and more–to some of the larger department stores such as Henri Bendel, Saks and Nordstrom. But now they sell some of the same pieces direct to customers – at a much lower price. The cheery and colorful two rooms display everything well and you want to buy all of it: cheaper bangles in the first room while the pricier jewelry such as the "statement necklaces" are in the back. "We're like a rock concert in here," one of the saleswomen said to me, trying to convey the excitement and the amount of people crowded around the jewelry. Indeed, just look at the excited faces of the shoppers! Or forget the shoppers and just look at the jewelry.

NOTE: There's a second SEQUIN OF PALM BEACH on Worth Ave at 219. They tend to have higher prices and bigger names, and more Badgley Mischka jewelry, while the iconic designers have their own shop nearby on the street. Sequin has a third spectacular shop now on the corner of Atlantic and Federal at 445 East Atlantic Avenue.

FIVE PLACES OTHER THAN WORTH AVENUE WORTH VISITING (THAT DON'T CARRY CLOTHES)

1) GREEN'S PHARMACY OF PALM BEACH is at 151 N. County Road, just a few blocks from the Sunset consignment shops, and next to a great takeout food emporium, Amici Market. This old-fashioned pharmacy has modern drugstore supplies, gifts and newspapers. But it also has history. The coffee-shop style restaurant was where John F. Kennedy regularly had breakfast.

2) MAIN STREET NEWS at 255 Royal Poinciana Way sells out-of-town newspapers, magazines, books, cards, cigars and gifts. "Popular items with the locals are our gag noses, pencil mustaches, mega eyebrows, and fake noses," says owner, Tommy Morrison. "Palm Beach people wear them to costume parties." Or at least that's why they claim they're buying them.

3) TROPICAL FRUIT SHOP at 261 Royal Poinciana Way could be the best-smelling place you've ever been to. Go there and take a whiff. Florida's oldest fruit shipper has the most wonderful aroma. They'll ship oranges to your friends up north who aren't lucky enough to be in Palm Beach like you are. Rub it in. (The thought; not the oranges.)

4) CLASSIC BOOKSHOP OF PALM BEACH is at 310 S. County Rd. In addition to a great selection of fiction and non-fiction books, in the center aisle are a large number of out-of-print books at greatly reduced prices.

5) The PALM BEACH BOOKSTORE, at 215 Royal Poinciana Way, in addition to a great selection of fiction and non-fiction books, has the largest section in Florida of books on interior design and architecture.

AFFORDABLE ART

Where can you buy original art these days? Not necessarily a gallery any more. So few of them are left, that an increasing number of artists are bringing their work into consignment places directly to sell their paintings. The galleries themselves are consigning what they don't sell, and people are bringing them in who own the art and want to make some money or redecorate.

Palm Beach Gardens

(NOT TO SCALE)

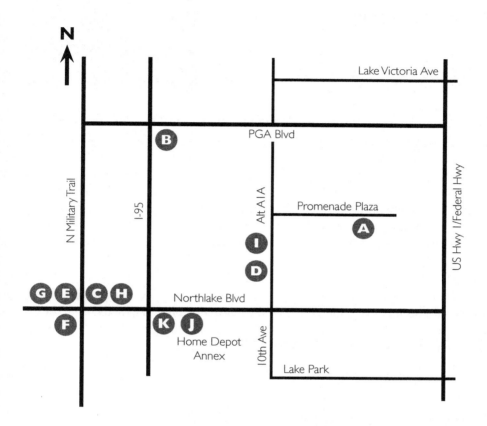

A.... Gwen's Consignment Connection (p. 86)

B..... Interiors Showroom (p. 86)

C.... Jennifer's Designer Exchange (p. 87)

D.... Ladies Choice (p. 87)

E..... My Friends Closet (p. 88)

F..... Oh Yeah Thrift Shop (p. 88)

G.... Resale Therapy (p. 89)

H.... She Shells (p. 90)

I....... Teapots & Treasures Café (p. 90)

J....... Treasures for Hope (p. 90)

K.... True Treasures Northlake Annex (p. 91)

GWEN'S CONSIGNMENT CONNECTION

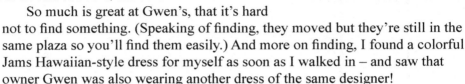

www.gwensconsignmentconnection.com
Promenade Plaza / 9850 Alt A1A Suite 509
Palm Beach Gardens 33410 / (561) 627-6076
OPEN: Mon.-Fri. 10-6; Sat. 10-5

So much is great at Gwen's, that it's hard not to find something. (Speaking of finding, they moved but they're still in the same plaza so you'll find them easily.) And more on finding, I found a colorful Jams Hawaiian-style dress for myself as soon as I walked in – and saw that owner Gwen was also wearing another dress of the same designer!

What's here for you? Chico's-philes will find a revolving rack of Chico's. Lilly-philes will appreciate all those Pulitzers. Recessionista fashionistas will gravitate to the less expensive everyday clothes in the back. Those searching for harder-to-find plus-sizes can't miss the racks of 18+ clothes. (Size, not age.) And those searching for new clothes will find some – with the original tags still on them!

For those bad at math, or who don't want to waste time calculating when they could be shopping, the labels on the garments tell you exactly what they will cost on which day. (So much easier than trying to figure it out. "Let's see, it came in on April 10th, it's been here 34 days, it should cost…")

FURNITURE (CONSIGNMENT)

INTERIORS SHOWROOM LLC

www.interiors-showroom.com
Oak Plaza Mall / 4118 PGA Blvd. / Palm Beach Gardens 33410 / (561) 622-4100
OPEN: Mon.-Sat. 10-5

They offer a wide variety of consigned furniture, with many recognizable names. The furniture looks new, but is only slightly "previously owned," and the prices are more than reasonable. Several major furniture stores are across the street with new pieces. But you'll see the same names at Interiors Showroom – at far lower prices – like Baker, Century, Drexel, Thomasville, Maitland, Smith, and Kreiss. Some items may not look quite as pristine when you buy resale, but after you've used a couch or chair a few times, it won't look brand new then either. So save your money for the housewarming party.

WOMEN'S CLOTHING & ACCESSORIES (CONSIGNMENT)

JENNIFER'S DESIGNER EXCHANGE

www.jennifersdesignexchange.com
Facebook: Jennifers Designer Exchange
4401 Northlake Blvd. / Palm Beach Gardens
33410 / (561) 459-7644
OPEN: Tues.-Sat. 10-5:30

All I can say about Jennifer's is "Where have you been all my life?" Well, my shopping life anyway, and I missed it because Jennifer's Designer Exchange just opened. There isn't a lot in the Palm Beach Gardens area for consignment nuts, so this large luxury shop is a wonderful addition. In fact, for those looking for higher-end consignment, it is definitely worth a trip just to come here.

Jennifer herself is not only friendly – not at all snobby – but knowledgeable, having once been the National Retail Director for designer apparel at Nordstrom. And now her shop ranks up there with the best. and priciest. This large airy shop carries all the high-end designers in perfect condition, and, yes, most of it is expensive–but exquisite. And probably never worn.

WOMEN'S CLOTHING & ACCESSORIES (CONSIGNMENT)

LADIES CHOICE

9339 Alt A1A, Suite #7B / Palm Beach Gardens 33403
(561) 881-0302
OPEN: Tues.-Sat. 10-5:30

You think of the word "jewel" the minute you walk in and look around – even before you learn that the owner's name is Jewel! She's owned this small but lovely shop for 21 years, during which time it has earned its excellent reputation by selling consistently attractive and trendy women's clothes at surprisingly low prices.

Another bonus is that it's very easy to navigate and you won't be tripping over clothes and struggling to find what you want. The rows of clothes – including a few sexy garments! – can be found in racks down the middle and sides of the store. Accessories are in the middle, and also in a showcase near the sales counter. All stores should be this well laid out and attractively stocked! **SHOP NEARBY:** TEAPOTS & TREASURES. (See p. 90)

WOMEN'S CLOTHES (CONSIGNMENT)

MY FRIENDS CLOSET

4595 Northlake Blvd. / Palm Beach Gardens 33418 / (561) 622-3600
OPEN: Mon.-Fri 10-6; Sat. 10-4

This is a friend you want to have! This is a "closet" you want to visit. Regularly. Often. You'll find it in the back of this lovely mall that already carries an outstanding home décor shop, (see RESALE THERAPY p. 89)

Once you walk in, you'll see that everything is neatly organized not only according to size and type but also price, so you can hang out in the less expensive alcove, or visit the large upscale room to the right. Or you can ooh and aah over the things in the Accessories Room straight ahead, and also in the front area, all neatly separated, making it easy to dive into what you want. For example, in the Accessories Room, there's a section of leopard skin, another of all green, and an area of new or almost new shoes. Lisa, the owner's enthusiasm for the merchandise in her four-year old shop is contagious. She promises – and it's true – that they sell everything from Macy's to Valentino's, from small to size 2X, from affordable to high-end labels, and it's all lovely to look at (better to buy).

The prices are good, and they're even further reduced depending on when the garment came in. And that's what you should do: come in.

CLOTHES, FURNITURE & MISCELLANEOUS (THRIFT)

OH YEAH THRIFT SHOP

8091 N. Military Trail / Palm Beach Gardens 33410
(561) 799-4870
OPEN: Mon.-Sat. 10-7

Where on earth did this place get that name? (It used to be SUNNY'S SECOND CHANCE, named after the owner, whose name, naturally, was Sunny.) But the new owners a year ago must have been struggling for a name, came up with one, and said "Oh yeah,that's it," But they forgot what the name they had just come up with was, so they just named it "Oh Yeah." Or maybe they mean "Oh yeah, let's go there." Who knows. It's certainly different. The shop.... not so much.

For whatever reason they named it, the layout is simple: the clothes are to the left and include women's, men's and children's apparel. The more expensive boutique clothes are in the middle of the room to the left as you enter. Household items are in the middle room. The room to the right has furniture.

SPECIAL SALES: Tuesday is up to 50% off for veterans; Every day 25% off for seniors (55+)

SHOPS NEARBY: GOODWILL PALM BEACH GARDENS BOUTIQUE at 4224 North Lake Blvd.

HOME DÉCOR (CONSIGNMENT)

RESALE THERAPY

www.resaletherapyshoppe.com
4595 Northlake Blvd., Ste 113 / Palm Beach Gardens 33418
(561) 691-4590
OPEN: Mon.-Sat. 10-5

Starting with its clever name, right down to everything in the shop, this place is outstanding. The row of almost ceiling-high trees in the center give it a lovely tropical look, and if you had to find any fault with this place it's that it's so packed with marvelous things that getting around is difficult.

It's almost overstocked with high-end, new and vintage merchandise including home décor, antiques, art and quality consignments, along with outright purchased items. You'll find accessories, cabinets, tables and desks, lighting, glass, china, rugs and more.

As for bargains, if you go to http:// www.resaletherapyshoppe.com/ coupon.htm, they often have a 20% off coupon for one item.

They also do room transformations, staging, design consultations, and professional organizing. And when you look at the job they've done to make this place beautiful, you can be confident that they'll do an outstanding job on your place as well.

SHOP NEARBY: While everything is new, not resale, the best new age shop in the county is a few doors down, and they have a lot of great things. And since you're at this mall anyway (for this shop and MY FRIEND'\S CLOSET in the back), you might as well visit JAMAR'S ENLIGHTENMENT CENTER at Suite 107.

They have a beautiful gift shop in the front room (the back is reserved for classes, with such top psychics as Michelle Whitedove). You'll find many wonderful and exotic gifts in this front room, along with handcrafted jewelry, paintings, statuary, healing stones, crystals and fascinating books like "The 100 Top Psychics & Astrologers in America."

SHE SELLS SEASHELLS

SheSellsSeashellsBoutique@gmail.com,
4376 Northlake Blvd. / Palm Beach Gardens 33410
OPEN: Tues.-Sat. 10-6

The name is adorable and so are a lot of the clothes and toys in this upscale children's consignment shop. It's new at this location (it was formerly in Lake Park) and everything here looks new (but it usually isn't). Unlike most children's consignment, they also have a lot of beachy things, as well as maternity, mom's-wear and handbags. (They don't have a listed phone number because they'd rather people contact them at SheSellsSeashellsBoutique@gmail.com

TEAPOTS AND TREASURES CAFÉ AND CURIOSITIES

http://teapotsandtreasurescafe.com
Oak Plaza Mall, 9339 Hwy. A1A, #10
Palm Beach Gardens 33403 / (561) 881-0447
OPEN: Tues.-Fri. 10-5; Sat. 11-5

Three charming areas in one: a restaurant, a gift shop – which also displays vintage as well as locally designed jewelry – and a furniture store. The little restaurant not only has great food – they serve "lunch, coffee, tea and decadent desserts," but present it on fine china with bouquets of flowers on each table. And you can buy the tables and chairs you're sitting on afterwards!

All around are gifts and knickknacks, and next door is a small furniture store next door with a separate entrance, is absolutely not to be missed. Not with all those quaint and whimsical eclectic furniture pieces and unique home accessories squeezed inside.

TREASURES FOR HOPE

www.treasuresforhope.org
3540 Northlake Blvd. /Palm Beach Gardens 33403 / (561) 691-8881
OPEN: Mon.-Fri. 10-6; Sat. 10-4.

This large stand-alone shop on Northlake came highly recommended to the Happy Shopper by a friend named Peggy who knows thrift shops. And when she said "this is one of the best thrift shops…" she knew what she was talking about. Indeed, during a check there, a furniture buyer was eyeing the unique and incredibly inexpensive (for what you're getting) unusual items you practically trip over, and she was positively swooning. "Whatever you say you can't say enough good things," she said to me.

With one exception: the clothes in a separate room were disappointing, very thrifty, and the few "boutique items," there barely warranted a second look.

But the rest of it…. Furniture like a white $10,000 Roche-Bobois couch in more-than-acceptable condition for $750. A group of Western home goods that included a rare real boot-lamp. Who knows what you'll find in this large thrift shop but as Peggy promised, it's good enough to warrant a special trip there. The only sad thing is that most of us don't have room to take most of it home.

Also unusual for a thrift shop: two alcoves of children's toys, clothes, and miscellany. This charity shop that provides jobs, training and mentoring opportunities benefiting Place of Hope and Villages of Hope could also provide you with a lot of inexpensive gently-used items for your home or closet. And help others at the same time.

FURNITURE & HOME DÉCOR (CONSIGNMENT)

TRUE TREASURES HOME DEPOT ANNEX

www.truetreasuresinc.com
Home Depot Center / 3926 NorthLake Blvd.
Palm Beach Gardens / (561) 694-2812
OPEN: Mon.-Wed. 10-6; Thurs.-Sat. 10-8; Sun. 12-5.

This immense 14,000-square-foot showroom is filled to the beautiful brim with attractive home furnishings. The merchandise isn't grouped according to type, so you pretty much have to walk through the whole place if you're looking for something specific. But you won't mind because it's a treasure to be at…. Oh, you know.

Incredibly, they have a $1 section – that's right – in a little corner in the back. You can scavenge through and find dishes, bric-a-brac, and even a small amount of clothes.

SPECIAL SHOPPING TOUR – WOMEN'S & CHILDREN'S RESALE CLOTHES IN TEQUESTA

Start at: Tequesta Fashion Mall at 150 US 1. There you'll find **TEQUESTA STOCK EXCHANGE**, a woman's consignment shop at #19. (See p. 94)

SNOOTY HOOTY'S also at 150 US 1 (#23) is a vintage and everything fun shop (See p. 94)

If you're looking for children's clothes, **FOREVER YOUNG** is #7 in the same mall. (See p. 93)

CLOTHES & MISCELLANEOUS (THRIFT)

ANGELS IN THE ATTIC

578 N. U.S. 1 / Tequesta 33469 / (561) 743-1275
OPEN: Tues.-Sat. 10-4

You might find a bargain at this budget thrift as well – I got my favorite Lalique-looking champagne glasses–for $3 each. Angels in the Attic is large, with a nice spacious feeling, and a variety of merchandise at rock bottom prices. The owner, Jean Immucci, has stocked it with children's clothes for $1, adult blouses for $2, books, and don't be surprised if you see that inside that crib – are golf clubs!

FURNITURE (CONSIGNMENT)

CLASSIC FURNISHINGS

www.classicfurnishings.net
Village Square Mall / 223 S. U.S. Hwy. 1 / Tequesta 33469 / (561) 575-7107
OPEN: Mon.-Sat. 10:30-5:30

Looking for patio furniture? Enamored of the Florida/Bahamas wicker-rattan-tropical look? Then this is the place for you. This family-owned-and-operated store has been in the business for over 30 years. Their two combined emporiums total 7,300 square feet, making it "one" of the largest furniture consignment stores in Palm Beach County. Actually, only about 30% of the combined two stores have consigned goods, but because of their total size, that still is more consignment furniture than you'll generally find elsewhere.

They pick up and deliver, plus they're one of the few places offering a buy-back guarantee for model rooms, usually set up by realtors and decorators. Classic Furnishings promises to repurchase (at 50% minus sales tax) what was paid for the furniture when it is returned.

CHILDREN'S CLOTHES & FURNITURE (CONSIGNMENT)

FOREVER YOUNG CHILDREN'S CONSIGNMENT INC.

Fashion Mall, 150 N. U.S. I, Ste. 7
Tequesta 33469 / (561) 746-3776
OPEN: Tue.-Fri. 10-5; Sat. 10-4

Two "Kims," Kim Choynowski and Kim Robbins, own this large, bright, and cheerful boutique which opened in January, 2009. They carry gently used children's clothing from newborn to size 6, maternity clothing, nursery furniture & equipment, toys, books, DVD's, new dancewear, new infant and toddler swimwear, and new baby gift items.

A BONUS: A special area for children to play in while their parents are shopping

CLOTHES & MISCELLANEOUS (THRIFT)

PENNIES FOR HEAVEN THRIFT SHOP

Church of the Good Shepherd / 400 Seabrook Rd. / Tequesta 33469
(561) 746-4674 x112
OPEN: Tues.-Fri. 9-4; Sat. 10-2

Volunteers and shoppers sometimes call this "Tequesta's best kept secret" because of the merchandise offerings and prices. This thrift and boutique with the clever name belongs to the Episcopal Church of the Good Shepherd, and it's one of the oldest thrifts in the county. It's been around for 40 years, and is located just off the courtyard on the church grounds.

They carry mostly women's clothing and accessories, although they have some select things for children, and men's clothing options too. On one recent inspection, a nicely lined sports coat was selling for $7.50–fully lined.

WOMEN'S CLOTHING & ACCESSORIES (RESALE & VINTAGE)

SNOOTY HOOTY'S

150 U.S.1, Suite #23 / Tequesta 33469
(561) 747-2400
OPEN Mon.-Sat. 10-6

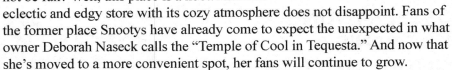

How can any place called Snooty Hooty not be fun? Well, this place is a hoot. And this eclectic and edgy store with its cozy atmosphere does not disappoint. Fans of the former place Snootys have already come to expect the unexpected in what owner Deborah Naseck calls the "Temple of Cool in Tequesta." And now that she's moved to a more convenient spot, her fans will continue to grow.

So much is for sale, and it's such fun to browse, that the prices almost don't matter because you don't feel that you must buy something to be happy.

CONSIGNMENT SHOP NEARBY: TEQUESTA STOCK EXCHANGE (See p. 94)

WOMEN'S CLOTHING & ACCESSORIES (CONSIGNMENT)

TEQUESTA STOCK EXCHANGE

Facebook: Tequesta Stock Exchange Inc
Tequesta Fashion Mall / 150 U.S.1, Ste. 19 / Tequesta 33469
(561) 746-0046
OPEN: Tues.-Sat. 10-5

The name "stock exchange" is a clever one for a clothing (ladies consignment) shop, but the real "stock exchange" is a place where you might lose something, namely your money. This stock exchange is one in which you have to come out ahead if you buy something because everything is great and the price is more than right.

This bright attractive shop is small, but its range of women's clothes is not. I don't know how they get so much great merchandise in here without your feeling crowded but they do. It's one of the best-known best-liked consignment shops in the area. It's certainly one of my favorite in the whole northern part of the county. The selection is exciting – it includes many Lilly Pulitzers – and the prices are excellent. It's also comforting not to feel squeezed in when you're browsing. The owner, Linda O'Loughlin, is another reason people come here, and come here they do. Even when other shops are empty (and complaining), people just seem to be arriving. If you do the same, you'll soon see why.

West Palm Beach – South Dixie Highway

(NOT TO SCALE)

N ↑

Belvedere Road

Southern Boulevard

Dixie Highway

A.... ARC (p. 96)

B..... Animal Rescue League Thrift Store (p. 97)

C.... Aristokids Outpost (p. 98)

D.... Cashmere Buffalo (p. 98)

E..... Celebrity Consignments (p. 99)

F..... City Girl Consignment (p. 100)

G.... Dina C's Fab & Funky (p. 101)

H.... Dina C's Fab & Funky For Men (p. 101)

I....... Nearly New (p. 102)

J....... Nettie's Consignment (p. 103)

K.... One More Time! Thrift Shop (p. 103)

L..... Palm Beach Vintage (p. 104)

M.... Resale Boutique (p. 104)

95

SPECIAL DIXIE HIGHWAY (IN WEST PALM BEACH) SHOPPING TOUR – ONE MILE OF CONSIGNMENT, THRIFT, VINTAGE, ANTIQUE & HOME DÉCOR SHOPS

Near Belvedere almost to Okeechobee on Dixie Highway are a series of shops too few bargain shoppers know about – but they should. They're located right outside of Palm Beach, and the merchandise may be the same but the prices are often much lower.

Start at: **CITY GIRL CONSIGNMENT**, a women and children's consignment shop is at 1900 S. Dixie Hwy. (See p. 100)

NEARLY NEW is an upscale thrift shop at 2218 S. Dixie Hwy. (See p. 102)

CELEBRITY CONSIGNMENTS at 1930 S. Dixie has beautiful home décor and antiques (See p. 99)

ANIMAL RESCUE LEAGUE THRIFT STORE at 1905 S. Dixie Hwy. (See p. 97)

DINA C'S FAB & FUNKY BOUTIQUE at 1609 S. Dixie Hwy., Ste.#2, is a high-end women's consignment shop. (See p. 101)

FOR MORE SHOPS IN WEST PALM BEACH, SEE BELOW.

ANTIQUES

ARC

www.antiquerowconsignments.com
3636 S. Dixie Hwy. / West Palm Beach 33405 / (561) 822 3382
OPEN: Mon.-Sat. 10-5

ARC, which stands for Antique Row Consignments, is the only large antique gallery in the famous Antique Row section of West Palm Beach. Although it's large enough to be one, it's not a dealer's emporium. The advantage to those is that with many sellers, there's a large variety in merchandise and pricing. But all the antiques here are owned by one person, although he's filled the beautiful interior with attractive and mostly expensive antique pieces for the home.

The prices are what you would expect for high quality merchandise, although there are a few sale items interspersed throughout. If you're looking for a bargain, go to their back tent, which you can enter through the store, or directly from the street through a parking lot between Dixie and Olive. It's a small hard-to-get-around area, and everything there – mostly chairs and furniture with a smattering of clothes – is half off.

A tent – or a 50% off section – is not what you'd expect in a place like this. And something else unexpected is.... Liz Lippman. Many of us remember – and liked– her from her years on Lake Avenue with the OFF THE WALL Shop and wondered where she was. Well, she's here.

You'll find her on the second floor, where there's 300 square feet of vintage clothing and accessories. Her two rooms are filled with clothes, shoes and jewelry, plus she has a a second "boutique" area that's even higher-end vintage.

Downstairs is a display case that's another "Liz section," consisting of stunning costume jewelry and unusual jeweled handbags.

NOTE: Directly across from the back tented area is a tiny mall, with a restaurant you shouldn't miss: Belle & Maxwell's at 3700 South Dixie. Great food – especially the carrot cake!

Clothes, Furniture & Miscellaneous (Thrift)

ANIMAL RESCUE LEAGUE THRIFT STORE
www.hspb.org / Facebook: Peggy Adams ARL
1905 S. Dixie Hwy. / West Palm Beach 33401 / (561) 833-8131
OPEN: Mon.-Sat. 9-6

Buy one of the thrifty treasures here and you could be saving the life of a dog or cat. So what are you waiting for? Many lovely pieces regularly come in to the Peggy Adams Animal Rescue League Thrift Shop, especially in the furniture and boutique departments, so it's not difficult to find something nice to buy from them.

A few racks of better clothes (for men and women) plus shoes at surprisingly low prices are concentrated right past the counter. There are some incredible bargains here. I saw a gorgeous one-of-a-kind robe/caftan for $20. Shortly thereafter, I saw it in another upscale shop–for $95. That gives you an idea of the value of some of the boutique items. (And sure, they probably purchased it from Animal Rescue.)

WHAT'S ON SALE: 20% off for seniors (55+) on Wednesday.
PARKING: A lot is in the back.
CONSIGNMENT SHOP NEARBY: DINA C'S FAB & FUNKY. (See p. 101)

CHILDREN'S CLOTHING (OUTLET)

ARISTOKIDS OUTPOST

www.aristokids.com / Facebook: aristokids.post
6003 S. Dixie Hwy. / West Palm Beach 33405 / (561) 547-1737
OPEN: Mon.-Thurs. 11-4; Fri. 1-6; Sat. 11-4

How would you like to buy great children's clothes from the town of Palm Beach at half the price? Then come to this small Dixie Highway outlet shop, which offers 50% off brand new children and adult clothes from Aristokids, Girls Club, and Boys Club at 07/307a/309 South County Rd., in Palm Beach.

Newborn, children and junior clothes are all represented in the racks. And squeezed next to those is a full rack of men's clothes to size 42; a revolving rack of miscellaneous sportswear for adult women; shoes; and bathing suits, cover-ups and more – all at half price. Or more.

ANTIQUES

CASHMERE BUFFALO

www.cashmerebuffalo.net
3709 S. Dixie Hwy. / West Palm Beach 33405 / (561) 659-5441
OPEN: Mon.-Sat. 10:30-5

This smallish shop is included in this book not because there are any bargains here, which there aren't, but because they have so many unusual items that it's worth popping into, especially if you're at the large catty-corner antique shop, ARC (See p. 96)

Simply from the name of this place (what the heck is a cashmere buffalo?) you know you're going to find weird things. And this 20-year-old shop does not disappoint. One room is "mod," the other "antiquey," and they promise not only the standard furniture, lighting, jewelry and linens, but also "textures & inspirations, little luxuries, and objects of desire." Nice.

My husband says if I keep shopping, he'll leave me. I'm going to miss him.

FURNITURE & HOME DÉCOR (CONSIGNMENT)

CELEBRITY CONSIGNMENTS

1930 S. Dixie Hwy. / West Palm Beach
33401 / (561) 578-4340
OPEN: Tues.-Fri. 11-5; Sat. 11-3.
Closed in the summer.

This is a hard-to-describe shop so you'll just have to go in – it's right across the street from Animal Rescue League Thrift Store – and see all the wonderful things here for yourself. You may also see someone who looks familiar and yes, you're right. He's the owner. But you'll be so busy trying to decide where in your home you could put some of the finds, that your attention will soon be diverted.

You'll be occupied wandering around, admiring the eclectic assortment of wonderful furniture, art and accent pieces. Like the stunning large Japanese screen that was there during a recent visit. Also, wall sconces that previously hung in a 1928 Paris hotel. Vintage Mardi Gras items. Old Louis Vuitton steamer trunks. And an elephant statue in the corner that confirmed that the man you saw was who you thought it was.

Women usually love what they buy,
yet hate two-thirds of what is in their closets.

BARGAIN SAVING TIP: ANTIQUE SHOPS VERSUS MALLS

Price-conscious shoppers are more likely to find a bargain in a mall than in a regular antique store. In a mall, dealers may offer lower prices because the competition is right there. If it's too expensive, or not quite what you want, you can easily move on to another booth. In addition, sadly, a few exhibitors are always going out of business, and you can find some bargains in their booths.

WOMEN'S & MEN'S CLOTHES (CONSIGNMENT)

CITY GIRL CONSIGNMENT

www.citygirlconsignment.com
1900 S. Dixie Hwy. / West Palm Beach
33401 / (561) 820-0075
OPEN: Sun.-Fri. 10-5:30; Sat. 10-4

How do we love thee? Let us count the ways? First, City Girl has the most beautiful assortment of women's consignment clothes and accessories. Then there are their prices, some of which are so low for what you're getting that it's hard to believe. Add to that a large shop with many rooms and a great assortment to choose from in many ranges, from the casual separates to upscale (but never outrageously expensive) gowns to a large selection of belts to handbags that go from totally affordable and charming to Chanel behind a glass counter. There's so many exciting clothes and accessories here – including a large selection of Lillys and a small section of men's– all nicely displayed and separated according to type with room to wander around.

It's almost impossible not to find something to fall in love with here.

And that includes owner Tami, whom everybody loves.

Once we all loved the original City Girl, which was housed in a beautiful three-room 1920's shop, with a cute bicycle built for two on the front lawn, and a fireplace in the main room. We all thought consignment shops couldn't get better – until Tami moved to this larger place allowing her to stock more merchandise, for more age ranges with clothes appealing to everyone, including teens and college students.

This place is, as the expression goes, to die.

And, oh yes, it's color coded so the already low prices are often even lower.

THRIFT SHOP NEARBY: If you go north, slightly past Belvedere on the east side of the Street is a pink awning. There's a great thrift shop there, NEARLY NEW (See p. 102) and you can park in the back.

" I always say shopping is cheaper
than a psychiatrist"
– Tammy Faye Baker

WOMEN'S VINTAGE & CONTEMPORARY CLOTHES & ACCESSORIES (CONSIGNMENT)

DINA C'S FAB & FUNKY BOUTIQUE

www.fabandfunkyvintage.com / Facebook: fabandfunky
"The Gatsby Building" / 1609 S. Dixie Hwy., Ste.#2
West Palm Beach 33401 / (561) 659-1420
OPEN: Mon.-Sat. 12-6

One of the best-liked women in Palm Beach opened up a high-end consignment shop that has rapidly become a very well-liked shop. I have been coming here since Dina opened a few years ago, and have never seen an item here anyplace else. You can't say that about what's in most consignment shops!

Dina herself dresses uniquely, in fab and funky, of course. She tells you that she's not looking for – nor does she wear – clothing and accessories that "are made in China."

Not only is Dina's place unique, so is her family. Besides her two adorable schnauzers, her daughter, Lily, at the age of 10 became internationally famous after appearing on David Letterman and major magazines for her talent of hypnotizing and dressing up the local lizards. They were then photographed, and thus developed into a cottage industry of greeting cards and T-shirts. Of course, you can find Lizard-Ville products stocked here as well. And the little girl has grown up and is sometimes at the counter as well.

SHOP NEARBY: Norton Museum of Art at 1451 S. Olive Avenue.

MEN'S CLOTHES (CONSIGNMENT)

DINA C'S FAB & FUNKY FOR MEN

fabandfunkyvintage.com
1609 S. Dixie Hwy. Suite 3 / West Palm Beach 33401 / (561) 659-1420
OPEN: Mon.-Sat. 12-6, Sun. 1-5 (in season)

We all love Dina C's Fab & Funky for Women, for while it isn't inexpensive, they have some of the most beautiful items (especially costume jewelry) you'll find in a consignment shop outside of Sunset Avenue in Palm Beach where the prices are much much higher.

Their new next door shop for men actually has quite a bit of sale items for women as well. You'll find women's shoes at 50% off, plus jewelry trays and purses on a table for like $20, plus a rack of better clothes for $50 and next to it one for $100.

But what's really unique is that it's one of only three places in two counties that sell contemporary (as well as vintage) high-end men's clothes and ties, luggage, and more. (The only two other upscale consignment shops are THE MAN CAVE in Tequesta and SOME MEN LIKE IT HAUTE in Fort Lauderdale. (See p. 136)

Dina carries everything from vintage to current, with names like Zegna, Pucci, Lilly, Graham, Cardin, etc. Not only will you find men's better shirts and jackets here, but Versace ties for $95. They recently got dozens of Maus & Hoffman unworn shirts, which they were selling for $35 in the back.

WOMEN'S MEN'S & CHILDREN'S CLOTHES, FURNITURE, JEWELRY & MISCELLANEOUS (QUALITY THRIFT)

NEARLY NEW

www.morsegeriatric.org/giving/thrift-shop.php
Facebook: Nearly New Shop
2218 S. Dixie Hwy. / West Palm Beach 33401
(561) 655-3230
OPEN: Mon.-Fri. 9:30-5; Sat. 9-4; Sun. 12-4

If I could only go to one shop ever it might well be this one. I've been coming here for years and I can practically never leave without buying something – and feeling I got a great buy to boot. Most of what's in my shopping bag afterwards are clothes or accessories, but when I moved to Florida (from NY) I even bought a beautiful framed Peter Max painting (in the back is the furniture and art, although some stunning pieces are also placed at the entrance as well) for $4,500. And it was appraised right afterwards for $7,500 – without a frame. But it's the smaller stuff that should make this a big place on your list. (And it supports a good charity: MorseLife, which the Joseph L. Morse Geriatric Center is part of.)

Bottom line: Nearly New is a marvelous upscale thrift; clean and much bigger than it looks because of a large separate room in the back for furniture, paintings and an alcove for boutique clothes in the back, along with a men's department section up front. It's got a little bit of everything, most of which is vastly superior to what you find in a thrift store. Especially outstanding are the women's suits, dresses, handbags and shoes, all at excellent prices. In addition, they always have sales going on and racks at practically give-away prices–making most things here a true bargain. Plus, the manager here, Susan, is one of the best.

NETTIE'S CONSIGNMENT

Facebook:/Netties Thrift Consignment
5404 S. Dixie Hwy. / West Palm Beach 33405 / (561) 202-7211
OPEN: Mon.-Sat. 11-6; closed Thurs., Sun.

Don't let the junky-looking outside (usually filled with chairs and low-end furniture) turn you off and prevent you from entering and looking around. They purchase the contents of estates: mostly furniture, artwork, and jewelry, vintage and custom. They then sell the antiques and some collectibles to walk-ins, decorators, designers, and dealers. Prices ranging from $1-$10,000 for merchandise within the 5,000-square-foot space.

HOME DÉCOR SHOP NEARBY: PALM BEACH HOME COLLECTION at 6207 S. Dixie Highway has a lot of interesting décor and accent pieces with many finds under $100, some way under. It's right near the famed Antique Row but with far more affordable prices.

ONE MORE TIME! THRIFT SHOP AND COFFEE BAR

www.thelordsplace.org
7600 S. Dixie Hwy. / West Palm Beach
33407 / (561) 494-0125 #6
OPEN: Mon.-Sat. 9-5

Would you like to go to a thrift shop where their boutique items are occasionally donated by rich Palm Beach women? Then come on over to South Dixie's One More Time, which supports an important charity: The Lord's Place. They carry some budget clothes and miscellaneous household goods in their six sparkling-clean rooms where, by the way, everything is easy to find because it's in separate areas. And what you buy helps the homeless in this county.

Highly unusual: they have a separate electronics room, which includes TV sets, DVDs and more. Another unusual thing: not only are there clean and tidy men's and ladies' rooms available, but they're one of the few stores to have a separate one for special needs or handicapped customers.

PALM BEACH VINTAGE

www.palmbeachvintage.com / Facebook: Palm Beach Vintage

3623 S. Dixie Hwy. / West Palm Beach 33405 / (561) 718-4075

OPEN: Nov.-Apr. Mon.-Sat. 11-5; May-Oct. Fri. and Sat.12-5; other times by appointment.

Calling itself "A Palm Beach secret since 1978," the shop sells vintage couture and designer clothes in one large room, with women's upscale designer vintage classics all around the sides – and some stunning accessories in the middle.

Louise Pinson explained that: "My vintage is custom or ready to wear, American or European, one-of-a-kind designer and renegade, one season wunderkind, from the 1800's through the 1980's and a little later, and occasionally something sneaks in from Chanel or Dior, or who knows who."

But don't go looking for sale specials. The owner explains that she doesn't have sales "because what we have is difficult to find and it goes up in value."

RESALE BOUTIQUE

ctrfam.org

319 Belvedere Rd. Unit 6 / West Palm Beach 33405 /(561) 899-3331

OPEN: Mon.-Sat. 10-5.

This relative newcomer is right off Dixie, and even though they have a nice ambience (the large window extends throughout most of the store so it's bright and airy) and they have okay prices, they may have problems getting a foothold. It's not that easy to find and there's not that much foot traffic here.

You're unlikely to just stumble upon it since it's between Olive and Dixie on Belvedere (most of the traffic there is going to Jojo's Sushi), and it's in the near corner of the eastern part of the small two-section mall. You can't see it from the street, so they'll pretty much have to count on word of mouth and/or repeat business. But both will hopefully sustain them since this is a nice addition to the Dixie consignment shops between Southern and Okeechobee.

The ample 3,000 square feet contains three rooms, with plenty of space for furniture, (a few larger pieces), decorative household items, (pillows, picture frames, end tables), artwork, an occasional antique, gift items, books & DVDs, clothes, or whatever comes in. There's still enough merchandise to warrant a slight detour to get here.

West Palm Beach, Wellington & More

(NOT TO SCALE)

N ←

Dixie Hwy/US 1

Georgia Ave

I-95

Congress Ave

AIRPORT

N Military Trail

Jog Road

Royal Palm Bch Blvd

Florida Turnpike

Okeechobee Blvd

Belvedere Road

Southern Blvd

Forest Hill Blvd

US 441/SR7

W. Forest Hill Blvd

Wellington Trace

A .... Abused Women's Thrift Boutique (p. 106)

B ..... Antique and Collectibles Show at South FL Fairgrounds (p. 106)

C .... Connie's Collection Consignment (p. 107)

D .... Consign and Design (p. 108)

E ..... Gratitude House (p. 108)

F ..... Hospice: Resale Shop Central (p. 109)

G .... Kofski Estate Sale (p. 109)

H .... On Course Consignment (p. 110)

I ..... Red Balloon of Wellington (p. 110)

ABUSED WOMEN'S THRIFT BOUTIQUE

7110 S. Dixie Hwy. / West Palm Beach 33405 / (561) 586-1888

OPEN: Mon. 12-3; Tues.-Sat. 11-4

This is a large, dark, and heavily stocked thrift shop, but there's something really depressing about this place, and that includes the people you see shopping there. They claim that good consignment/thrift shops regularly donate their name brand clothing to them, but a few checks have never turned up anything worth touching, nonetheless buying.

They do carry a few things most thrifts don't, for example, food at the back of the big large main room, plus a lot of well-priced linens in the smaller back room. There are even a few good items behind the cash register, but those aren't the prices you'll see elsewhere and are not enough to warrant a trip.

You might be tempted to come here after the nearby WORLD THRIFT, or ONE MORE TIME, but try to resist the temptation.

SPECIAL MONTHLY SALE | ANTIQUE

ANTIQUE AND COLLECTIBLES SHOW AT THE SOUTH FLORIDA FAIRGROUNDS

www.americraftcenter.com/calendar.php

9067 Southern Blvd. / West Palm Beach 33411 / (561) 793-0333

OPEN: On the first Friday, Saturday, and Sunday of every month.

For the last 18 years, the popular West Palm Beach Antique and Collectibles show is held at the Americraft Expo Center, Generally on Friday and Saturday from 9-5 and Sunday from 10-4:30.

The monthly fairs are held in two large indoor rooms, and a small outdoor section, where there are often some good buys, especially around the periphery. Don't miss the one in mid-February, when they have their annual giant Winter Spectacular and over 1,000 indoor and outdoor dealers come from all over the country.

NOTE: Thrifties might also want to keep their eyes when the Fairground has occasional one-day garage sale, which are fun and often rewarding.

HOW TO GET THERE: It's located off Southern Boulevard in West Palm Beach, 1.5 miles west of the Florida Turnpike and 1 mile east of 441/SR7.

BACK ON THE RACK

http://pbbackontherack.com

219 S. Olive Ave. / West Palm Beach 33401 / (561) 835-0006

OPEN: Tues. Sun. 10-8.

Nice consigned clothes and accessories at really low prices. Some new mixed in at 25% off. Everything reduced after 30 days. Always four racks of 50% off. Another rack of half off shoes. Customer appreciation cards with discounts after you spend a certain amount. Even open on Sunday. It sounds like consignment heaven. Except for one thing: location, location, location. It isn't in the heart of downtown (it's on the northwest corner of S. Olive and Evernia Street), and parking isn't easy. And when you can find space, you've got to deal with meters. Still, this new shop is worth a visit, but if you do go, bring quarters.

SHOP NEARBY: CLEMATIS STREET BOOKS & CAFE at 206 Clematis Street is a wonderful shop with quirky cards and great books, sweets, coffee and a real old-time General Store atmosphere you won't find elsewhere any more. Come here to see it, as well as see what's in it.

CONNIE'S COLLECTION CONSIGNMENT BOUTIQUE.

www.conniescollection.com

9859 Lake Worth Rd. / Wellington 33467 / (561) 964-0990

OPEN: Mon.-Sat. 10-6

If you're anywhere within many miles, then detour here. Or make a special trip. There are nice labels, for example, plenty of Lilly Pulitzers and Chicos. Even furs in the winter. A recent check turned up a blouse with the Loehmann's Back Room tag still on it, which Loehmann's had reduced to $69, down from an original $220 and here at Connie's it was $17!!! Also around were hard-to-find, one-of-a-kind unusual handbags by Mary Frances, Lulu Guinness, and Paloma Picasso, all in perfect-looking condition! All this plus plenty of bargains and clearance racks in the back.

That said, run, do not walk, to this place (OK, drive), as soon as possible. It's a wonderful women's consignment shop, and the prices are lower than at some comparable consignment shops.

CONSIGN AND DESIGN OF WELLINGTON

www.myconsignanddesign.com / Facebook: Consign And Design Wellington
13857 Wellington Trace / Wellington 33414 / (561) 798-5222
OPEN: Mon.-Fri. 10-6; Sat. 10-5

This place is expensive, but everything is negotiable and they have occasional sales, like their anniversary sale the last week of August-Labor Day and another Memorial Day sale, when everything is 20-75% off.

They do have a lot of lovely things to look at and lots of it in the 4,000 square foot showroom, which claims to be the largest high-end furniture consignment and antique furnishings store in the whole area. Another reason to go: if you're into horses and knickknacks and pillows with pictures of them on it, you'll enjoy all the equestrian accessories and décor.

DECOR ONCE MORE

http://www.decoroncemore.com,
6758 N. Military Trail, Fairfax Center / West Palm Beach 33407
(561) 840-8858)
OPEN: Mon.- Sat. 10-7; Sun. 11-5

Lots of what you'd expect, and a bit of what you wouldn't expect, like the Caribou Taxidermy Full Shoulder Mount ($1,195), perfect for people who want others to think they're out shooting these cute creatures instead of buying furniture.

This woman-owned estate-buying store carries lots of high-quality lightly and slightly-used furniture, from vintage to modern with some occasional bargains, like coffee tables for $50.

GRATITUDE HOUSE

1700 N. Dixie Hwy. / West Palm Beach 33407 / (561) 833-6826
OPEN Tues.-Fri. 10-4

This large thrift shop is hard to find and probably not worth it once you do. The address is on the building so that part is easy.... but the entrance.... where is it? And where in heck are you supposed to park your car?

If you decide to brave it–it's a quarter of a mile north of Good Samaritan Hospital–you'll see that 99% of the stuff is definitely el cheapo. In quality and price. For example, women's blouses are $2-3 but who would want them?

Up front, however, in what they call the "Boutique Section" (such as it is), there are occasional huge bargains. For example, a brand new evening gown with a $2057 price tag hanging from it was on sale for $135, which was also the highest price item there by a wide margin. A Mondo men's shirt (and they have a bit of men's and a small amount of furniture, housewares, and knickknacks) that sells for $90 was there for $4 – but required some cleaning.

So die hard thrifties (and dealers) might want to scout this place out for an occasional bargain – if they can find the entrance.

CLOTHES, FURNITURE & MISCELLANEOUS (THRIFT)

HOSPICE: RESALE SHOP CENTRAL

www.hpbc.com/resale
1324 N. Military Trail / West Palm Beach 33409 / (561) 681-6511
OPEN: Mon.-Sat. 10-5

Many good deals are to be found in this large clean-looking four-room thrift, which is heavily stocked with two rooms of smart contemporary furniture at good prices. You can also often find TV sets, sometimes even large screen ones, in the corner of the furniture section. The other areas feature clothes, accessories, and miscellany, all nicely set out so you don't feel cramped or crowded as you wander through the felicitously priced goods.

SHOP NEARBY: WALMART SUPERCENTER is one-half mile away at 4375 Belvedere Rd., Goodwill West Palm Beach Clearance Center is nearby at 1897 Old Okeechobee Road.

SPECIAL SALE | ESTATE

KOFSKI ESTATE SALE

http://kofskiantiques.com
5501 Georgia Ave. / West Palm Beach 33405 / (561) 585-1976
OPEN: From Dec.-May, approximately every 6 weeks. Check website.

Eager bargainers and determined dealers line up in the early morning hours, and by 10, a lot of the merchandise may have been sold. But the facility is huge – 12,000 square feet consisting of two ample-sized rooms, an outdoor area, and "The Marketplace" across the street – so come on down.

The atmosphere is very festive – when a piano is for sale, someone may be playing it – so it's more like a party than a sale. But then too, a sale is always a reason to party.

The inventory changes constantly, but includes large and small furniture pieces and home décor. Prices may start around $6 and go to thousands for antiques and decorative arts.

SALE INFORMATION: Many people don't realize that on Monday, if the merchandise didn't sell and is still available, it may be had for a better price, since Kofski is more open to negotiation at that time than at the height of the weekend.

HOW TO GET THERE: From Dixie Hwy., turn west on Bunker Rd. It's on the corner of Bunker and Georgia between Southern and Forest Hill.

EQUESTRIAN (CONSIGNMENT)

ON COURSE CONSIGNMENT SHOP

http://wellington-wef.com/on_course/business.html
Facebook: On Course Consignment Wellington
Wellington Plaza / 12773 W. Forest Hill Blvd., Suite 110 / Wellington 33414
(561) 753-6256
OPEN: Mon.-Fri. 10:30-5:30; Sat 10-6. Open Sun.

Could there be a successful consignment shop devoted to used equestrian tack and riding apparel for children as well as adults? Neigh-sayers (ha ha!) might say "No." But in Wellington, Florida, horse country, one can indeed find such a place.

So trot on down to "On Course," a small shop with interesting paraphernalia for the horse owner, rider, or just plain horse lover. They carry saddles, bridles, riding coats, jackets breeches, boots, children's riding apparel, blankets, ribbons, and cookies. For the horse, not the rider.

CLOTHES CONSIGNMENT & ACCESSORIES

RED BALLOON OF WELLINGTON

www.shopredballoon.com / Facebook: red balloon consignment
Kobosco's Corner Shopping Center 9120 Forest Hill Blvd.
Wellington 33411 / (561) 333-2515
OPEN: Mon.-Fri. 10-6; Sat. 10-5:30

Just 8 miles west of their landmark store in West Palm Beach, Red

Balloon has a not-to-be missed second location in Wellington. This gem is conveniently located near the Wellington Green Mall on Forest Hill Blvd. It offers amazing new boutique and designer couture and like-new trend labels at great prices. Like their landmark store, they have attractively low prices for what you get. NOTE: Wellington also has a Goodwill Boutique at 13873 Wellington Trace and a Plato's Closet with teen-centric clothes at 10200 Forest Hill Boulevard #110.

HOME DÉCOR & GIFTS (CONSIGNMENT)

THIS N THAT
www.thisnthatwpb.com
216 Clematis St. /West Palm Beach 33401 /(561)833-5223
OPEN: Tues. Wed. Fr. 11-7; Thurs. 11-10; Sat. 10:30-6; Sun. 12-5

This place is a delightful surprise. First of all, who would have thought there would be a lovely affordable home décor- small furniture type place amidst all the entertainment venues here?

The size of it is also a nice surprise, because there's only a small window on the street (don't miss it) making you think it must be a really tiny place. But inside, it's long and narrow so the size of it and how much is in there is a pleasant surprise. It's also nice and bright, which you also don't expect with only one small window to the street.

But the best surprise is all the wonderful things inside– and at a terrific price. A lot of it tagged quite low, and even the more expensive items. For example, during one visit there was a huge Eiffel Tower screen at only $295, and obviously worth much more.

Besides the furniture, there's everything from paintings to handbags making browsing fun, and rewarding, since you'll definitely find interesting things to look at and probably to buy.

So don't overlook This N That, especially on a Saturday when you can also go to the nearby Green Market which runs from 8-2. (Don't miss the Chowder Heads Stall for their delicious lobster rolls and hard-to-find Rhode Island clam chowder.)

While you're here, you should also stop at CLEMATIS STREET BOOKS & CAFE a few doors down at 206 Clematis Street, and since This N That is open late, you can also drop by when you're taking in one of the great shows at the nearby Palm Beach Dramaworks Theatre, or dining at one of the many terrific nearby restaurants. (Oli's, Santucci, Longboards)

PART 2:
BROWARD COUNTY

Including

WEST OF FORT LAUDERDALE......................113
(Coral Springs, Plantation & Sunrise)

SOUTH OF FORT LAUDERDALE....................119
(Cooper City, Davie, Hollywood
& Pembroke Pines)

DEERFIELD BEACH 123

FORT LAUDERDALE................................127

OAKLAND PARK & WILTON MANORS.........132

POMPANO BEACH 138

Broward - West of Fort Lauderdale
(Coral Springs, Plantation & Sunrise)

(NOT TO SCALE)

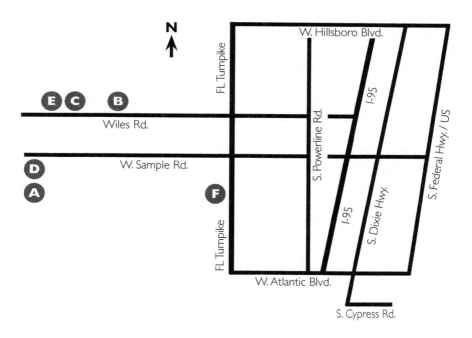

A .... Merri-Go-Round (p. 114)

B ..... MonkeyzKloset (p. 114)

C .... Nannie's Vintage (p. 115)

D .... Sawgrass Mills Outlet Stores (p. 116)

E ..... Stash Boutique (p. 117)

F ..... Twice But Nice (p. 118)

MERRI-GO-ROUND

6906 Cypress Rd. / Plantation 33317
(954) 791-8320
OPEN: Tues.–Sat. 10-5

Like the Merry-go-round its named for, Merri-Go-Round is a colorful consignment shop. It has a large variety of clothes in a wide range of fashions with great variation in prices. There is always a $5 rack — for example, containing shoes — and something like a Jimmy Choo bag for $695 that was here when I was checking them out. I spotted some tags for heavy-hitter designers around. There were handbags even hanging on the walls above the clothes racks and lots of jewelry up front; some quite nice. Mostly, I saw garments like a blouse that sells for $42 retail here for $19 and in perfect like-new condition. Cache slacks were $45. There were also some good sales, like two 60% off racks of handbags and shoes.

SHOPS NEARBY: TWICE BUT NICE. (See p. 118.) In addition, five minutes away at 8601 W. Broward Plvd., (954 792-7414) is a tiny but lovely shop run by FRIENDS OF THE WEST REGIONAL LIBRARY (Broward County). It's a gift shop with amazing prices for small pieces – attractive jewelry, scarves, small bags, that sort of thing. It's open Monday and Tuesday from 12-6, Wed.-Fr 11:30-5:30. It's in the library – and right near a section of books for sale.

MONKEYZKLOSET

www.monkeyzkloset.com.
7400 Wiles Rd., Suite 105 / Coral Springs 33067 / (954) 282-8275
OPEN: Tues.-Fri. 10-5:30; Sat. 10-4; Sun. 12-4.

They've been in the business 12 years now, and originally opened the shop to raise funds to adopt a child when they couldn't have one of their own. They thought. But four and six years later, Mom gave birth to Zoey and Kieran, and the Z and the K in MonkeyzKloset stands for them and is not an affectation.

Most of what's here is consigned clothes and standard children's fare, but this shop also strives to help local moms. They give them a showcase with a special section of hair accessories, flip-flops, shirts and more, all made by locals.

MEN'S, WOMEN'S & CHILDREN'S VINTAGE CLOTHES,
HOME DÉCOR, GIFTS & JEWLERY

NANNIE'S VINTAGE

Facebook: NanniesVintage
7880 Wiles Rd. / Coral Springs 33067
(954) 796-2101
OPEN: Tues.-Sat. 10:30-5

Nannie's offers so many good things for so many people in their four sections. "We've Got the Bling," is their motto, and you can see everywhere that bling is their thing. Up front is a lot of vintage, especially handbags and jewelry. Then, take a few steps down to the back section and there's a whole new world of mostly women's (and a few men's) clothes at double-take prices. A Dolce & Gabbana top for $15? An Adrienne Vittadini sweater for $9? Is this for real? It is. Nannie's is attracting a loyal clientele with these low, low prices.

But there's more than just a vintage clothes shop here. As you enter is a modern and very unvintagey looking jewelry store. They not only sell watches (including Rolexes), custom designed rings, and silver charms, but they also do jewelry and watch repair on the premises. So while you're waiting for them to fix something for you, you happily can kill time by going through all the wonderful fare the rest of this shop has to offer. Because there's even more. To the left is another large area with small furniture, knickknacks and interesting home décor you won't find elsewhere.

HOW MANY SHOES DO YOU OWN?

The average woman owns 19 pair of shoes and she bought her first pair without her mother at the age of 14. And even now she's pretty independent – or sneaky – about her shoe purchases, because one-quarter of the women admitted that they didn't tell their partners when they purchased another pair.

The survey, conducted by gocompare.com said that women will end up buying 469 pairs of shoes in their lifetime, spending close to $25,000 on them. (Presumably, those buying at consignment or thrift will spend less!)

So if you've bought close to 469 already, well, you were just setting yourself up for the rest of your life. But don't tell your partner about it.

RETAIL DISCOUNT OUTLET

SAWGRASS MILLS OUTLET STORES

www.simon.com/Mall/?id=1262 / Facebook: SawgrassMills
12801 W. Sunrise Blvd. / Sunrise 33323 / (954) 846-2350
(800) FLMILLS
OPEN: Mon.–Sat. 10–9:30; Sun. 11–8

This wonderful 173-store outlet mall (which houses such well-known stores as **Super Target, Brandsmart, JCPenney, Nike Factory Store, Burlington Coat Factory, American Signature Home, Bed, Bath & Beyond, TJ Maxx, Chico's Outlet, Gap Outlet, Sports Authority, Books-A-Million** and more) has plenty of bargains in each and every one of the shops.

True, some of the merchandise is last year's (who cares?) and some of it is made especially for malls and outlets (again, who cares), but you can still find great goodies everywhere. It's best to arrive when it opens and get out by 2 when it gets really crowded – especially on a holiday or big shopping day.

The information booths often sell a book of discount coupons. Look at it carefully and figure out if it includes places you plan to go to. (While you're here, ask for a map.) The mall is divided into colors (yellow, purple, red, green & blue) making it easy to find something in a particular section

If you're looking for luxury, the back outdoor section, The Oasis, has a **Nordstrom Rack** with clothes from the department store. (**Off 5th Saks Fifth Avenue Outlet Store** in the indoor mall, tends to puff up and fill in their inventory with specially made lower-quality merchandise more than the other major department stores here.)

The second luxury area is up front, and the distance is so great you may even want to repark your car to get here. The Colonnade outlets have all the heavy-hitters, like **Burberry, St. Johns, Coach, Barney's Department Store.** In the Colonnade is also the **Nieman Marcus** (widely known as Needless Markup) **Last Call** store, with genuine merchandise from their store jammed together at greatly reduced prices. In back of Nieman's, where they have the gifts and furniture, is an exit. If you cross over, you'll stumble upon a great **Marshalls**. Some say the best in Broward is in Coral Ridge but this one is terrific, too.

"Sweater . . . garment worn by child when its mother is feeling chilly."
– Ambrose Bierce

116

WOMEN'S CLOTHING & ACCESSORIES (CONSIGNMENT)

STASH BOUTIQUE

www.stashboutique.net
Facebook: shopstashbique
8200 Wiles Rd. / Coral Springs 33065
(954) 575-1075
OPEN: Tues.-Sat. 11-6.

It took a while but Stash finally arrived – and this place is really worth waiting for! It has a stunning interior that looks like a cross between a South Beach and a Soho shop. And everything is all spaced out nicely so you don't feel at all crowded in this medium-sized boutique.

Only about half is consignment and the rest is retail, which includes several lines that you won't find anyplace else in the US. But all of it is well (meaning affordably) priced, and so beautiful, you'll find yourself pulling out a lot of things to look at closer and try on.

The jewelry is also outstanding, and there are some well-priced (designer) handbags here as well.

Jacki Rosen, the owner, also plans on selling "museum-quality" paintings along one of the walls.

This place has already been voted the best boutique in Coral Springs and Parkland. One step inside and you'll agree.

FURNITURE, HOME DÉCOR & ACCESSORIES (CONSIGNMENT)

THE CONSIGNMENT POST

www.theconsignmentpost.com
9661 W. Sample Rd. / Coral Springs 33065 / (954) 340-7171
OPEN: Tues.-Sat. 10-5:30

For those looking for "upscale treasures at unbeatable prices," that just happens to be the motto of The Consignment Post. (It's also a clever name for a shop whose owner/designer is named Lori Post.) They carry upscale furniture, lighting, accessories, antiques, collectibles, designer handbags and better costume jewelry– and some things are always on sale there. By the way, they also have an elegant Royal Tea Room located inside the shop for private parties.

TWICE BUT NICE

5229 W. Broward Blvd. / Plantation 33317
(954) 581-6423
OPEN: Tues.–Fri. 11-6; Sat. 11-5

I first saw this store through the window – when it was closed – and I immediately wanted to return. Not only could I see beautiful clothes inside, all laid out nicely, but in the window was a brand new Michael Kors handbag with the sales tag still dangling from it: $349. When I squinted, I could see that it was here for $180.

Once I returned and entered, I saw that many of the new items in this shop were discounted even more, sometimes as much as one-third. (About 20% of the clothes and accessories here are new.) The resales often had even more impressive markdowns and were often in almost pristine condition, including a few higher-end handbags like Coach. I also found a lot more plus size clothes in this tiny but very full shop than I find at most consignments. *Two* racks of them in fact.

Another thing that's unique for a consignment – they carry *real* jewelry (gold, vintage, antique, and sterling) as well as the standard costume.

SPECIAL SALES: Check the *SunSentinel* under "Garage Sales" for their once a month 25% off sale.

CONSIGNMENT SHOP NEARBY: MERRI-GO-ROUND. (See p. 114.)

Never wear anything that panics the cat.
– P.J. O'Rourke

TIP: BUYING WALKERS AND WHEELCHAIRS AT A DISCOUNT

If you've ever (unfortunately) needed a walker, or a wheelchair, crutches or a cane, you know how outrageously expensive they can be in a medical supply or drugstore. But thrift shops connected to hospitals (e.g., Jupiter Medical Center, Debbie-Rand) usually have a lot of them.

Broward - South of Fort Lauderdale
(Cooper City, Davie, Hollywood & Pembroke Pines)

(NOT TO SCALE)

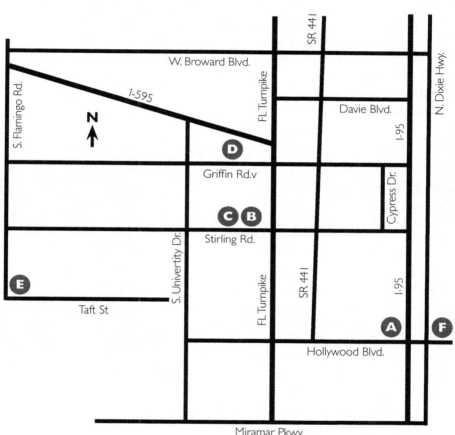

A.... American Thrift Store (p. 120)
B..... Another Chance (p. 120)
C.... Another Chance Home Décor (p. 121)
D.... Cooper City (p. 121)
E..... Kidz Exchange (p. 122)
F..... Two Timer (p. 122)

WOMEN'S, MEN'S & CHILDREN'S CLOTHES & HOME GOODS (THRIFT)

AMERICAN THRIFT STORE

www.shopamericanthrift.com

330 S. State Rd., 7 / Hollywood 33023 / (954) 962-4983

OPEN: Mon. 10-6; Tues. Thurs. 9:30-6; Wed. 9-6:30; Fri. 9:30-7:30;
Sat. 10-5:30; Sun. 11-5

There are two American Thrifts in Broward County, and the other is at 5051 N University Drive; Lauderhill. They've been around almost 20 years and the large rooms are stuffed with lots of used – a lot of it looks VERY used – clothing (women's, men's, children's), toys, household goods (linens, furniture, mattresses), electronics, antique and collectibles, art gallery, and an impressive book section.

WOMEN'S CLOTHING & ACCESSORIES (CONSIGNMENT)

ANOTHER CHANCE

Victoria Plaza 6125 Stirling Rd.
Davie 33314 / (954) 584-5150

OPEN: Tues. - Fri. 10-5; Wed. 10–7;
Sat. 10-4; Sun. 12-4

Sometimes when I'm down this way and I only have time to go to one shop, I end up at Another Chance. It's rapidly become one of my favorites with its friendly owner Karen and its really nice selection of women's and teens' consignment clothes. That includes some big-name designer handbags and shoes over to the right past the checkout counter, where better accessories are offered at impressive (meaning good) prices.

There's a lot throughout but it doesn't feel crowded, so you can comfortably walk around and look at all the clothes that are attractively displayed. I once had to wait out a blinding rainstorm, and found things I had missed in the medium–sized area even after close to a half-hour here.

Karen always finds time to chat with her many customers – she has 4,000 active accounts!–and she's very knowledgeable about this business which she's been in for 16 years. "Give people quality and good prices and they'll come back .... and back." I always do – and so do many others.

They're open Wednesdays until 7, and every week they have "Wine

Wednesdays" when they serve wine to the eager shoppers. Just another example of how they go the extra ounce, er, mile for their happy customers.

SALE INFORMATION: There's a 75% off rack the first week of every month as well as the rack in the back that's always discounted.

FURNITURE, HOME DÉCOR & MEN'S CLOTHES (CONSIGNMENT)

ANOTHER CHANCE - HOME DECOR

Victoria Plaza 6133 Stirling Rd. / Davie 33314 / (954) 584-5150
OPEN: Tues. - Fri. 10-5; Wed. 10–7; Sat. 10-4; Sun. 12-4

Just four doors away from Karen's popular women's clothing consignment and accessories (see above), she's opened up a second shop for furniture, home décor (they were previously in the other shop) and that rarity in the consignment world, men's clothes. Although this shop has just opened – on the 17th anniversary of her being in this business – already her sense of style evident in the women's consignment shop can be seen here. So this is sure to be a great place.

ANTIQUE MALL

COOPER CITY ANTIQUE MALL

www.coopercityantiquemall.com / Facebook: Cooper City Antique Mall
9800 Gifffin Rd. / Cooper City 33328 / (954) 252-0788
OPEN: Mon.-Sat. 10-6; Sun. 12-5

I was destined to like any place named Cooper (since that is my maiden name) and they didn't disappoint. From the moment I walked in I felt like I was in a beautiful new world. "The dealers display their wares, they don't just toss them in," explained Claudia Cayne, one of the owners.

Not surprisingly, a lot of pickers and set designers come here and they can easily photograph and work with the exhibits because almost all are open. Which gives it a nice airy feeling, as well as letting you easily touch and look as items you're considering buying.

Besides the cornucopia of fine quality antiques and collectibles throughout the 10,000 square feet, they offer design/decorating services, they will help you put together an estate tag sale, they buy gold and silver, offer an online wish list, have a few artists in residence specializing in repurposed art plus so much more. If that's possible.

CHILDREN'S CLOTHES & FURNITURE

KIDZ EXCHANGE

http://thekidzexchange.com
Facebook: The Kidz Exchange Consignment Store
12171 Taft St. / Pembroke Pines 33026 / (954) 435-5305
OPEN: Mon.-Fri. 10-6; Sat. 10-5

The oldest consignment shop in Broward County caters to the youngest residents. This large store for little ones has everything from newborn up – and it's easy to find whatever you want. "We're known to be extremely well organized for easier shopping," said owner Judi Mckissick. "Girls on one side and boys on the other." They must be doing something right – for the last 28 years – because for the last dozen, they've won the prestigious *Parents* Magazine's "Best of the Best" kids consignment store.

About 25% of what's here is brand new, and at about 40-50% below retail. In addition to clothes for girls and boys to size 16, they also have dance wear, uniforms, strollers, swings, nursery furniture, cribs, high chairs, books, and more. They offer some pick up services if you want to consign cribs and larger nursery furniture.

WOMEN'S CLOTHING & ACCESSORIES (CONSIGNMENT)

TWO TIMER

2325 Hollywood Blvd. / Hollywood 33020
(954) 923-8501
OPEN: Mon.-Fri. 10-5; Sat 10-4

Once upon a time, Hollywood was filled with consignment shops. Now, only this one remains. Fortunately, this one is large, a two-part store with a wide selection of women's clothes and accessories. Plus some housewares and objects of art, children's things, and everything from Barry Manilow handbags to college football towels. So browsing is fun, even if the prices aren't always as low as some of the other consignments.

But you'll often encounter various selections on sale which brings the prices down. Unfortunately, you can't always figure out what's on sale. Color tags sometimes mean it's reduced, and color dots mean. Well…. You'll just have to ask. Fortunately, the owner, Pat, is friendly and helpful.

So, while this is all that's left, for the consignment freak, it's enough.

Deerfield Beach

FURNITURE, HOME DÉCOR, JEWELRY & CLOTHES (CONSIGNMENT)

A CONSIGNMENT GALLERY DECORATIVE ARTS MALL

www.aconsignmentgallery.com
Facebook: a consignment gallery
350 S. Federal Hwy. / Deerfield Beach 33441 /
(954) 421-2395
OPEN: Mon.-Sat. 10-6; Sun. 12-5.

The first time I came here – and I now visit regularly – I thought I had died and gone to (consignment) heaven. Everything is so wonderful – and there's so much of it. This place is so large that if you go with a friend, make sure you both have cell phones. You'll probably have to find each other at some point, since this is the largest consignment shop in Southeast Florida.

Actually, it's really two places, with a combined 32,000 feet. The left-hand side is the individually owned (for over 20 years) consignment gallery with fine furniture, home accessories, lighting, books, clothes, jewelry, or whatever they happen to get in.

When I first checked it out, they had received an estate with vintage and gently used clothes. In the latter category, an Escada silk blouse was marked $30 and they were giving a 20% off discount on clothes that day. At all times, they have some fabulous jewelry–costume as well as real–at excellent prices.

They have two entrances to the gallery. The right side is for the Decorative Arts Mall where they rent out booths to dealers. Other than having individual owners, the two sections are similar in terms of what they offer. As one visitor said: "You could furnish a city with this store. It's large, eat before arriving, and bring your wallet, as you will buy!!!!!"

SHOPS NEARBY: GOODWILL SUPERSTORE is across the street at 289 S. Federal Highway. Better still, if you're looking for home furnishing, travel a few miles away and go to A SUMMER PLACE at 131 E. Hillsboro Court. (See p. 124.)

FURNITURE, HOME DÉCOR & JEWLERY (CONSIGNMENT)

A SUMMER PLACE CONSIGNMENTS

www.asummerplaceconsignments.com
Facebook: A Summer Place Consignments
131 E. Hillsboro Court / Deerfield Beach 33441
/ (954) 426-6106
OPEN: Mon.-Sat. 10:30-5:30; Sun. 12-4.

This is another place that's always on the top of my list of spots to go to... again and again. Like A Consignment Gallery, this is a wonderful furniture and home décor spot in Deerfield Beach. They have ten-thousand square feet of old and new gently-used household furnishings, art, antiques, accessories, bedroom sets, glass and china.

It's a treat to walk through the many rooms because it's a gold mine of lovely furniture with good prices and friendly owners. (Look for Debbie). It's also in an interesting building. Indeed, it's one of the oldest in Deerfield Beach, and the rooms and nooks and crannies are great for placing all the wonderful pieces they bring in daily.

Make sure to stop by, and if you have the strength, combine it with a visit to A CONSIGNMENT GALLERY (See p. 123), and you will have a terrific – but exhausting – day. And you'll find so much, you'll never need to buy anything ever again. Sure.

Women's Men's & Children's Clothes (Thrift) & Home Décor

DEERFIELD THRIFT SHOPS

www.facebook.com/Deerfieldthrift
165 E. Hillsboro Blvd. / Deerfield 33441 & 1628 SE 3rd Ct.
Deerfield Beach, FL 33441 / (954) 871 -9632
OPEN: Mon.-Sat. 10-6, Sun. 11-4.

 A separate trip to the Deerfield Thrift Shop on Hillsboro is not recommended, but if you're at the nearby (and fabulous) furniture and home décor shop, A SUMMER PLACE (See p.124), you might as well do a little thrifting. You only need go to two places at this Deerfield Thrift: the front section to the left where they have the better clothes, and the back room where there are some antiques and collectibles. There are several other sections you can skip.

 The other Deerfield Thrift is in the Cove Shopping Center (near A1A in Deerfield), which is near another great home décor shop, A CONSIGNMENT GALLERY (See p.123). This Deerfield Thrift at the cove is smaller, brighter, and cleaner looking than the one on Hillsboro, and it has some decent home décor strewn around.

 Three pluses: In the same mall as the Deerfield Thrift in the Cove is one of the best Indian restaurants in Broward called Taj, and they have a great luncheon buffet. Secondly, the Deefield Thrift has been around for more than 25 years so they must be doing something good. And finally, the owner is very nice.

Women's Clothing & Accessories (Consignment)

THE SECRET GARDEN

Deerfield Plaza Mall / 3908 W. Hillsboro Blvd.
Deerfield Beach 33442 / (954) 426-0622
OPEN: Mon.-Sat. 10-6; Sun. 1–5

 It does look a bit like a garden when you walk in because it has a quaint atmosphere, and it's chock-a-block full of colorful clothes. You'd be hard put not to find something you'd like to look at more carefully, but there's so much that you should allow a lot of time for the hunt.

 Prices are OK (like $14 for an obviously not new Chico blouse, $24 for a Ralph Lauren sweater), and there's a nice 50% sales section in the back. There's also a lot of inexpensive jewelry around, and a few high-end handbags, e.g., $200 for a Michael Kors; $325 for a Gucci. There were also good buys on designer shoes: a real pair of Prada shoes in good condition were only $68; Tory Burch $79.

Bottom line: what's here is not unique but the atmosphere and layout is.

HAIL TO THE VEEP

You find strange bargains in thrift shops, as one man learned last year after purchasing a Brooks Brothers shirt for $1 in his local thrift. That would have been good enough. But when he unrolled the sleeves, cufflinks fell out. And they were gold. Making it even more valuable, they were inscribed as well: United States Senator Joseph H. Biden Jr. It appeared that the Vice President had donated his shirt to a thrift shop, forgetting that his cufflinks were still in it.

LOOKING FOR FURNITURE OR ANTIQUES? HERE'S THE BEST ANTIQUE/COLLECTIBLES/FURNITURE EMPORIUMS IN SOUTHEAST FLORIDA

If you're looking to furnish a house, with antiques or contemporary items, these are the places to go to, listed alphabeticlly (Christine will you alphabetize them – also I added one miami oner

A CONSIGNMENT GALLERY – Deerfield (See p. 123); *ANOTHER CHANCE - HOME DECOR – Davie (See p. 121) *A SUMMER PLACE – Deerfield (See p. 124); ALL GOOD THINGS – Lake Worth (See p. 53); BKG Galleries – Lake Worth (See p. 48); CAROUSEL ANTIQUE CENTER – Lake Worth (See p. 48); *COCONUT CONSIGNMENT COMPANY – Boca Raton (See p. 9); *CONSIGNMENTS BY SALLY – Lantana (See p. 59); HILLSBORO ANTIQUE MALL - Pompano (See p. 141); *JAMIE'S CLASSIC – Lantana – (See p. 60); *PALM BEACH HOME INTERIORS – Lake Worth (See p. 50); *PAST PERFECT – Boca Raton (See p. 19); *RESALE THERAPY – Palm Beach Gardens (See p. 89): TREASURES FOR HOPE - Palm Beach Gardens (See p. 90)

* This indicates that the place only carries contemporary furniture & home décor, no antiques.

Fort Lauderdale

(OAKLAND PARK & WILTON MAPS INCLUDED BELOW • NOT TO SCALE)

Fort Lauderdale

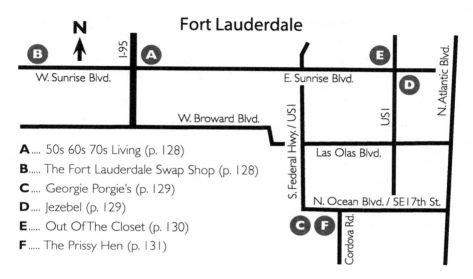

A.... 50s 60s 70s Living (p. 128)
B..... The Fort Lauderdale Swap Shop (p. 128)
C.... Georgie Porgie's (p. 129)
D.... Jezebel (p. 129)
E..... Out Of The Closet (p. 130)
F..... The Prissy Hen (p. 131)

Oakland Park

A.... Couture Upscale Consign (p. 132)
B..... Faith Farm (p. 133)
C.... Kids 'N Kribs (p. 134)
D.... Lidia's Consignment Closet (p. 135)
E..... My Sister's Closet (p. 135)
F..... Vintage Diversity (p. 137)

Wilton Manors

A.... Out Of The Closet (p. 130)
B..... The Poverello Center (p. 136)
C.... Some Men Like It Haute (p. 136)
D.... Worth Repeating (p. 138)

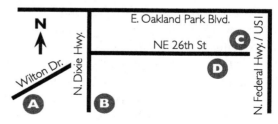

50s 60s 70s LIVING

http://www.50s60s70sliving.com/
1200 NE 4th Ave. / Fort Lauderdale 33304 / (954) 767-8000
OPEN: Mon.-Sun. 11am-6

They claim to have the largest selection of mid-century modern furniture, accessories, tables, seating, lighting "and all bits funky," they say. Lots of 1930s German style, 1950s- to 1980s American design and Lucite as well. They also rent everything in their stand-alone 2,500 square foot showroom for staging a home or shooting a movie.

Don't know what you want? Go to their website, click on "browse inventory" for the section you want, call them at (954) 565-5316, give them your credit card, and they'll ship it to you. One day we'll all shop for furniture – and everything else – like that.

THE FORT LAUDERDALE SWAP SHOP

Technically called the "Drive-in Theater, Carnival & Farmers' Market."
www.floridaswapshop.com
3291 W. Sunrise Blvd. / Fort Lauderdale 33311 / (954) 791-7927
Open: Mon. Tues. Wed. 9–5; Thurs. 7:30–6; Fri. 9-6; Sat. 7:30–6; Sun. 7:30– 6.

The *New Times* (www.Browardpalmbeach.com) called the Fort Lauderdale Swap Shop "The Best Tourist Trap" as well as the "Best Cheap Thrill" in Broward. I call it eBay meets a rummage sale. It's probably all so you may not want to miss it. Or maybe you do, especially if you listen to what some people who hate it say. "It's a yard sale for someone's moldy basement." And "Yes, there are bargains, but you need to be vaccinated before you go there."

As for the clientele, it's quite different from the (mostly elderly) people at the FESTIVAL (SAMPLE ROAD) FLEA MARKET. (See p. 139.) So be prepared. Weekends and in season are best but, of course, very crowded. If you do go, leave plenty of time, because you'll find it hard to visit all the booths in one day in this humongous place (just look it up on Google satellite map) containing new/used, and designer knock-offs in a third world setting.

They've been around for almost 50 years and were known as the Thunderbird Drive-In Movie Theater. They still have the drive-in but as one soul who braved it afterwards wrote: "Don't go to the drive-in there unless you are going to lock yourself in your car with tinted windows and you have a weapon. And totally out of the question to go to the bathroom because you might not make it back!"

CHILDREN'S CLOTHES (CONSIGNMENT)

GEORGIE PORGIE'S

http://www.gporgies.com

3045 N. Federal Hwy. / Fort Lauderdale 33306 / (954) 999-5450

OPEN: Mon.-Sat. 10-5

This children's consignment shop has just opened, so we'll have to wait a while to see whether the excellent level of merchandise at the beginning is maintained. But it looked promising. Now it's your turn to check it out.

WOMEN'S & MEN'S VINTAGE CLOTHES & ACCESSORIES + CARDS, BOOKS & GIFTS

JEZEBEL

www.ishopjezebel.com/1.html

1980 E. Sunrise Blvd. / Fort Lauderdale 33304 / (954) 761-7881

OPEN: In season, Mon.–Fr. 11-7; Sat. 11-8; Sun. 12 – 5.

This funky, adorable two-part shop is chock full of hip gifts, hilarious cards, stylish candles, unique home décor, vintage jewelry, T-shirts, candles, incense, soap, parasols, and everything in between. It's especially fun to go through the greeting cards, gift books, or humor books, like "How to Get Into Debt." (Many compulsive shoppers don't need any help in doing that.)

If you're not laughing too hard as you wander around, walk down a few steps where they have more fun fare – and the vintage that they're known for. That includes dresses, and assorted women's tops and bottoms, as well as men's clothes.

There's also a small amount of vintage in the front section, for example, those old Lucite bags, unusual (what would you expect here?) vintage jewelry, antique hats, and those weird cat's-eye vintage sunglasses that only the brave dare wear today.

They've been around since 1986 and they were voted the best boutique shop by the Broward *New Times*. That's easy to believe since they have some of the best (and funniest) merchandise you'll find any place in the county.

DON'T MISS: Boxes scattered around the floor that may contain 50% off things like greeting cards.

THRIFT SHOP NEARBY: OUT OF THE CLOSET on Sunrise Blvd. (See p. 130)

CLOTHES & MISCELLANEOUS (THRIFT)

OUT OF THE CLOSET

www.outofthecloset.org / www.ahf.org
Facebook: out of the Closet Thrift Stores
1785 E. Sunrise Blvd. / Ft Lauderdale 33304
(954) 462-9442
OPEN: Mon.–Sat. 10–7; Sun. 10-6

You can't miss this place with its bright pink
and turquoise front. And a good reason to shop here, besides the incredible
bargains, is that 96 cents out of every dollar you spend at any Out of the Closet
goes for the care and treatment of people living with HIV/AIDS.

But you may also want to shop here because of the amazing prices.
Blouses for $4. Men's shirts – and there are a lot of men's clothes here – for
about the same. Mostly it's what you'd find in any low-price or mid-range
thrift shop. But because of the charity, higher end items are sometimes
donated. (Frankly, though, most of the boutique items weren't great.)

In addition to clothes, you'll find lots and lots of home accessories (like
plates), decorative goods, picture frames, and miscellany (like rain hats), plus
a small selection of larger furniture, which is sparse and mostly unimpressive.

THRIFT SHOP NEARBY: The other Out of the Closet at 2097 Wilton Drive in
Wilton Manors. (See below.)

OUT OF THE CLOSETS IN SOUTHEAST FLORIDA

This California chain – all with the same can't-miss turquoise and pink
colors outside– are owned and operated by AIDS Healthcare Foundation
(AHF). Here are the Florida outlets.

FORT LAUDERDALE OUT OF THE CLOSET 1785 E. Sunrise Blvd. /
(954) 462-9442

MIAMI OUT OF THE CLOSET at 2900 N. Biscayne Blvd. /
(305) 764-3773

SOUTH BEACH OUT OF THE CLOSET at 1510 Alton Rd. /
(877) 259-8728

WILTON MANORS OUT OF THE CLOSET at 2097 Wilton Dr. /
(954) 358-5580.

WOMEN'S CLOTHING & ACCESSORIES (CONSIGNMENT)

THE PRISSY HEN

www.prissyhenconsignment.com
Facebook: The Prissy Hen
The Harbor Shops 1825 Cordova Rd.
Fort Lauderdale 33316 / (954) 462-4484
OPEN: Mon.–Fri. 10-6; Sat. 10-5; Sun 10-3 (call to check first)

With this odd name – from a 50's cartoon with a hen named Miss Priss who was always dressed with hats on – you'd expect a store that's very odd with funky, even weird clothes. Or maybe a children's consignment shop. But the Prissy Hen isn't prissy at all – just fabulous.

Expect to find–and you won't be disappointed–top-quality clothes for adult women: elegant separates, dresses, accessories, jewelry, and even a few nice gifts. Furthermore, if there's something specific you're looking for, go to their website, and enter it under "My Wish List," and they'll let you know if something that's begging to be bought by you comes in.

But besides their excellent merchandise, they also have positive vibes. "We're fun, friendly, and fabulous" says the owner, Linda, who has been running this place frequented by locals and tourists for the past eight years. "The hen had attitude and it's all about attitude," she says with a smile.

There's a small amount of retail and hard-to-find can't-live-without things like Hollywood tape (to keep those stray bra straps from showing). Among the new merchandise are also quality Pashmina scarves (excellently priced) and trendy sunglasses.

But mostly it's top-notch consignment from discerning locals. And it's open seven days a week.

So, The Prissy Hen is sure to leave you clucking with approval.

Shopping is a woman thing. It's a contact sport like football. Women enjoy the scrimmage, the noisy crowds, the danger of being trampled to death, and the ecstasy of the purchase.

Erma Bonbeck

Special Women's Clothing & Accessories Shopping Tour – Fort Lauderdale Area

Within a 12 mile stretch from north to south are four excellent consignment shops in Fort Lauderdale. From I95, exit Oakland Blvd., and go west to Federal Hwy.(US 1), and go south to COUTURE UPSCALE CONSIGN (See p. 132), housed in a green building that comes up quickly on the right.

Then drive three blocks south on Federal (US 1), turn right (west) on NE 26th Street to WORTH REPEATING (See p. 138).

From 1732 NE 26th St. Wilton Manors, head west toward NE 16th Ave. Take the 2nd left onto NE 15th Ave. At the trafic circle, continue straight to stay on NE 15th Ave. Turn right at Albert Gibson onto US1 S/E Sunrise Blvd. Continue and turn left onto SE17th St. Turn right onto Cordova and there's PRISSY HEN (See p. 131).

SEE BELOW FOR MORE SHOPS.

Women's Clothing & Accessories (Consignment)

COUTURE UPSCALE CONSIGN

www.coutureupscaleconsign.com Facebook:
Couture Upscale Consign
2939 N. Federal Hwy. / Fort Lauderdale
(Oakland Park) 33306 / (954) 565-4348
OPEN: Mon.-Sat. 11-6

They look almost like sisters, but they're a mother and daughter who together have made this two-room designer and couture upscale boutique quite unique. In their own words, they carry "today's hottest styles from top labels at a fraction of the retail price. That includes women's fashions, formal attire, casual wear, designer handbags, shoes and accessories."

As soon as you enter, you'll see their serious couture and high designer labels, such as Hermes, Chanel, Louis Vuitton, Gucci, Prada, Pucci, Roberto Cavalli, and more. But if it's less expensive that you're looking for, you'll find several reduced racks in the second room, which generally contains the less expensive clothes, shoes, and handbags.

SPECIAL SALES: In October, they have a "Breast Cancer Awareness" function. They also have seasonal sales which they advertise to those who subscribe to their mailing list, and also those who become Facebook fans.

HOW TO FIND IT: The store itself is painted green, but it's still easy to miss if you don't drive slowly, because it comes up around a slight curve on your right going south on Federal from Oakland Blvd.

UPSCALE CONSIGNMENT SHOP NEARBY: WORTH REPEATING (See p. 138)

CLOTHES, FURNITURE & MISCELLANEOUS (THRIFT)

FAITH FARM FORT LAUDERDALE CAMPUS AND THRIFT STORE
www.faithfarm.org
1980 NW 9th Ave. (aka Powerline)
Fort Lauderdale (Oakland Park) 33311 / (954) 763-7787
OPEN: Mon.–Sat. 9-6

Many of you thrifties know, like, and even frequent the Faith Farms in west Boynton Beach. So you may be tempted to try the one in Fort Lauderdale. Don't bother. You'll be turned off before you even go in. The neighborhood is iffy. The clientele outside may make you reach for your handbag. But the worst part is the overwhelming thrift smell as soon as you enter. When I visited – believe me only once – even the "better" items hanging on hangers had stains, and a nobody-washed-this-before-bringing-it-here look.

Sure, there are bargains. There are also awful-looking handbags for $3. Bric-a-brac that was often chipped or broken or the same cheap garbage you see everyplace, usually in better condition. Sure, bed spreads were only $10. But would you really want to risk bringing something like that into your home?

Stick with Boynton.

DON'T MISS: OK, if you feel you must come here, and are looking for a wedding dress, in back of the counter were a half dozen wedding dresses that looked quite nice. Really. When asked the price, the cashier said they were "from $250 to $150." Well, okay. The cashier is right at the entrance and you won't have to walk any farther in than the entrance to check out the gowns.

But if you buy one, be sure to have it cleaned before you bring it into your home.

SALE INFORMATION: Every Wednesday is Senior Day for people 55 & older. 25% off everything except new items or antiques. But who cares?

BARGAIN SPOT NEARBY: DRIVE-IN THEATER, CARNIVAL & FARMERS' MARKET (See p. 128)

OTHER FAITH FARM LOCATIONS: Boynton Beach Campus and Thrift Store, 9538 Hwy. 441, Boynton Beach, (561) 737-2222; Okeechobee Thrift Store, 1852 Hwy. 70, W. Okeechobee, (863) 467-4342.

CHILDREN'S CLOTHES AND FURNITURE (CONSIGNMENT)

KIDS 'N KRIBS

www.kidsnkribs93.com
1051 NE 45th St., (called Floranada)
Fort Lauderdale (Oakland Park) 33334
(954) 493-8697
OPEN: Tues.–Fri. 10–6; Sat. 10–4

This cheerful two-room shop has everything, and that means *everything*, for kids from the age of 0-14. The entire area has a nice finished look with its walls of blue and green. Up front (and also in the glass display by the checkout area), you'll find a small selection of brand new children's clothes.

But where are the cribs, excuse me, the Kribs in the name, you wonder as you wander around? Aha. In the back, to the left, is an entrance to a second room. There, you'll not only find cribs and bassinets, small beds and playpens, but just about any type of stationary furniture you could put in a child's room. There are also mobile conveyance for when you take the kids outside, like car seats and strollers. There are even a few things here you can't figure out what you do with them. Ah, sweet mystery.

A dress that zips up in the back will bring a husband and wife together.
– James H Boren

FOR CHANGES AND UPDATES TO THIS BOOK, SEE FACEBOOK: SHOPPINGINFLORIDA

LIDIA'S CONSIGNMENT CLOSET

5064 N. Dixie Highway / Fort Lauderdale (Oakland Park) 33334
(954) 771-0966

OPEN: Tues.–Fri. 10-5; Sat. 10-4

You'll find nice mid-range merchandise to go through. This small shop is heavily stocked with clothes and accessories–and somewhat uncommon for a resale shop–new cosmetics and unworn lingerie. There are also a few designer handbags in back of the counter at excellent prices (a Coach might be $50, Dooney & Bourke, $80) for those who don't demand that their bags look like they just came out of a retail store that day.

And speaking of bargains – and isn't that what we're here for? – you'll also find a $1 rack of great clothes that the consignor for some reason didn't want to take back. And it probably originally sold here for a lot more than that.

SPECIAL SALES: During the months of June and January, everything is 50% off.

MY SISTER'S CLOSET

www.sistersclosetboutique.com / Facebook: sisters closet
2665 E. Oakland Park Blvd. / Fort Lauderdale (Oakland Park) 33306
(954) 563–5559

OPEN: Tues. 10-6, Wed. 12-7; Thurs. 10-6; Fri. 10-5; Sat. 10-5.

This is not a big store but have they got big bargains! Over on the right, toward the back, are several 75% off "last chance" racks with lovely clothes that until recently were in the main part of the store at full price. And since their regular prices are in the $20-$40 range – although there are more expensive clothes around – you can imagine the bargains on these racks.

They also have a large selection of expensive attractive accessories, particularly designer handbags, costume jewelry, and sunglasses, most in an attractive little alcove in back of the counter.

Looking for jeans? They have as many as 100 pairs in here at any one time.

So this "sister" has high-end and highly affordable clothes and accessories to offer in her closet.

SPECIAL SALES: There's also a fill-a-bag sale after July 4th, and after Christmas. It's worth signing up here, because they have e-mail blasts to announce their specials.

UPSCALE CONSIGNMENT SHOP NEARBY: COUTURE UPSCALE. (See p. 132)

RESTAURANT NEARBY: There's a fabulous Four-Diamond award Chinese restaurant in this mall (at 2787 E. Oakland Blvd.,) called Rainbow Palace.

MEN'S CLOTHES (CONSIGNMENT)

SOME MEN LIKE IT HAUTE

www.somemenlikeithaute.com

2378 Wilton Dr. / Wilton Manors 33305 / (954) 561- 8650

OPEN: Tues. Wed. Thurs. 11-2 & 5pm-8 pm; Fri., Sat. 12-9; Sun. 12 noon-6

This is the only men's fine fashion consignment shop in Broward County – and one of only three in South Florida (See also DINA C'S FAB & FUNKY FOR MEN p. 101 & MAN CAVE p. 43) Behind an upscale storefront, in the heart of Wilton Manors, you'll find this elegant shop selling only new or very gently worn upscale designer shirts, shorts, tee shirts, pants, short sleeve shirts, and plenty of shoes, including sandals, sneakers, slip-ons, loafers and lace-ups, like Ferragamo, Gucci, Cole Haan, Prada and more.

In addition, this is the place to get those hard-to-find consigned accessories like men's sunglasses, belts, ties, cufflinks – and even luggage. From Armani to Zegna, they carry a wide variety of designers with many names that you know (and would like to own more of).

CLOTHES & MISCELLANEOUS (THRIFT)

THE POVERELLO CENTER

2056 N. Dixie Hwy. / Fort Lauderdale (Wilton Manors) / (954) 561-3663

OPEN: Mon. Tues. Wed. 10-4:40; Thurs. Fri. Sat. 10–6; Sun. 12-5

This is another thrift shop dedicated to helping people with HIV/AIDS – like the nearby OUT OF THE CLOSET (See p. 130). But this one helps by supporting a food bank for them.

At 10,000 square feet this is even larger than Out of the Closet, and like them, it's clean, and the clothes are presented nicely. With private closed dressing rooms. They sell everything here from big screen TVs to men's ties for $3, area rugs (in need of cleaning but for $5+ a good buy), mattresses, and lots and lots of housewares. And most importantly, they have good prices, like workout tops for a couple of dollars.

SALES INFORMATION: One-third off on Thursday and Friday.

WOMEN'S & MEN'S VINTAGE CLOTHES

VINTAGE DIVERSITY

vintagediversity.com
Facebook: Vintage Diversity Inc
236 W. Prospect Rd. / Fort Lauderdale
(Oakland Park) 33309 / (954) 566-7678
OPEN: Tues.-Fri. 12-6; Sat. 11-6

The unusual sights and sounds of days gone by provide a delightfully colorful atmosphere from the moment you walk into Vintage Diversity. Items in their 3,000 square foot showroom–unusually large for a vintage shop– are available for sale or rent from past eras of flapper to funky, and poodle to punk. It's very easy to find what you're looking for here, whether it is a purchase or rental piece, as items are clearly marked by size and era.

They have a vast inventory of '20's Flapper & '30's Gangster, 40's Wartime & Hollywood glamour, ' 50's Poodle skirts and bowling shirts, '60's hippie & Mod GoGo Girl, '70's Rocker or Disco Dancer, '80's Punk Rocker, Valley Girl, Surfer Dude and more. And each garment has been cleaned and repaired, restoring it to nearly new condition!

They also rent vintage clothing, costumes, collectibles and props for milestone birthdays, charity balls, reunions, anniversaries, showers, reunions, Bar/Bat Mitzvahs, theater, movies, photo shoots and commercials! They'll outfit you from head to toe, and the $120.00 costume rental includes everything from your wig to your shoes, and even sales tax. Kids sizes are also available for around $50.00. There are always items on bargain racks starting at $1.00!

SPECIAL SALE: Thrift Saturdays are "BOGO" Buy one item of clothing, shoes, or handbag and get the second for 1/2 price.

"I like my money right
where I can see it –
hanging in my closet."

– From the television show *Sex and the City*

WOMEN'S CLOTHING & ACCESSORIES (CONSIGNMENT)

WORTH REPEATING

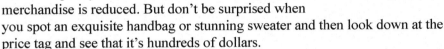

www.worthrepeatingfineconsignments.com
1732 NE 26th St. / Fort Lauderdale
(Wilton Manors) 33305
(954) 563–4443
OPEN: Mon.–Sat. 10-5

Worth Repeating Fine Consignments is worth (repeatedly) going to if you're looking for beautiful high-end clothes and accessories. Yes, there are some less pricey items mixed in when the regular merchandise is reduced. But don't be surprised when you spot an exquisite handbag or stunning sweater and then look down at the price tag and see that it's hundreds of dollars.

Considering the level of clothes here, it's no surprise to find large open "closets" containing all St. Johns: tops, dresses, pants, and pantsuits. The prices are excellent, especially when you consider what these clothes in just about the same perfect condition would cost at the real place. And there's more of them here!

This large well-lit well-stocked store is unusually full for an upscale consignment so you have plenty of great things to go through. Indeed, it's even larger than it looks at first because of a back area to the right that's filled with even more beautiful merchandise.

Finally, women have happily found it worth repeating their visits to this place worth repeating for 22 years. It's also in a lovely Colonial-front building, so this place is a knockout (with no knockoffs!) on the outside as well as in.

UPSCALE CONSIGNMENT SHOP NEARBY: COUTURE UPSCALE (See p. 132)

GILDING THE LILLY (PULITZER)

No designer is more quintessentially Palm Beach than its own Lilly Pulitzer. She started her career by running a fruit and juice stand. The bright pink, green, and pastel Lilly-look came about because she wanted colors and patterns strong enough to hide the stains when the food fell on her. Current Lillys can be found in many local venues, and a few places in this book sell her vintage line.

WOMEN'S CLOTHING & ACCESSORIES (CONSIGNMENT)

DÉJÀVU

www.dejavuconsignment.net

Garden Isle Shopping Center 452 S. Cypress Rd. / Pompano Beach 33060
(954) 942-5700

OPEN: Mon. 10-6; Tue.–Fri. 10-8; Sat. 10-6; Sun. 1-6

Said owner Rose Wilson, "We have everything from mink coats to bikinis." So, if you're looking for a place that has something for everybody, then this may indeed be the place for you. There's even a child-friendly front section for children – and it's put together and the merchandise is sold by the owner's 9-year-old daughter. "We have consigners from 15-98 – five generations shop here," she said proudly.

NOTE: Rose admitted that this place "might be overwhelming to some," so you can call her up in advance, tell her what you want, and she'll find it for you here.

SALE INFORMATION: 10% off to new customers, plus monthly sales.

FLEA MARKET

FESTIVAL (SAMPLE ROAD) FLEA MARKET

www.festival.com / Facebook: Festival Flea Market

Festival Flea Market Mall / 2900 W. Sample Rd. / Pompano Beach 33069
(954) 979-4555; (800) 353-2627

OPEN: Mon.–Fri. 9:30–5; Sat. Sun. 9:30-6

This is the best discount mall in the country – truly heaven for the bargain shopper who likes to flea. The only thing you won't find here are high prices – and the low prices are even better if you take advantage of their coupons. Look for them at their website, Facebook page, and in the *SunSentinel*. Or become a fan on their Facebook page, and they'll give you discounts and keep you informed of specials, too.

You can redeem them near the **Fiesta Pet Deli** (ST 430 Parade East.) Which, by the way, is a great pet shop. This veterinarian-owned pet shop, is the largest independent one in Broward County. They sell more than just packaged or canned dog or cat food and pet accoutrements. There's a weird-looking raw meat counter that looks just like what you'd see in a butcher shop for people – but it's for dogs.

At B0012 Broadway (there's a place to redeem coupons here too) is a wonderful cosmetics store called **Yonique Cosmetic Outlet & Fragrances**. You'll know you're in the right place when you see all the women milling around and lined up to check out. They have a huge inventory of brand makeup, hair products and expensive skin lotions, with sales clerks walking around to help you find what you're looking for. Gosh, just like in a real store. The bad part is there's only one checkout counter and usually a line. Next door is the popular **Rachel's** which always has a rack of inexpensive clothes at the entrance. They also have a petite and plus size area next to each other (so someone has a sense of humor) in the back.

After wandering all through the mall, your feet will hurt. This is a good time to buy comfortable shoes at a discount and the best place, **LAS Comfort** at ST160 Parade West, is right near Hanky Pankys.

Nearby is the **food court** with a choice of Jewish deli, Chinese, fried chicken, Philly Cheese steaks, Greek gyros and a couple of other cuisines. None of it very good. There's also a large **food market** nearby for fruit and other edibles at ST140 Parade West. which is good. And **The New York Pickle Company** small stand at B6717 is terrific.

The bad – and alas often the ugly – is the fact that row upon row carries the same thing at the same price. After a while, especially if you have the strength to cover all 500 shops, you get tired of the same endless low-end jewelry shops, phone accessory items, women's sequined T-shirts, etc. But just when you swear you'll never come back, you find one thing you've been looking for, or you spot something you needed, or you stumble upon an outrageous bargain, and then it's all worthwhile. And next thing you know, you come back again.

SHOPS NEARBY: THE HILLSBORO ANTIQUE MALL is part of the Festival Flea Market. (See p. 141.)

NOTE: You might want to check out another flea market in Broward County. The HOLLYWOOD DOG TRACK FLEA MARKET @ MARDI GRAS CASINO, 831 N. Federal Hwy., Hallandale Beach, (954) 454-8666, Their outdoor market opens Fri. Sat. Sun., November-April; Sat. Sun. May-October. It's been described as a "bad place in the summer; good in the winter."

HILLSBORO ANTIQUE MALL & CAFÉ

www.hillsboroantiquemall.com / Facebook: Hillsboro Antique Mall
2900 W. Sample Rd. / Pompano Beach 33073 / (954) 571-9988
OPEN: Mon.–Fri. 9:30–5; Sat. Sun. 9:30–6

The Hillsboro Antique Mall's 250 dealers (in 35,000 square feet) are looking to appeal to the shoppers at the flea market next door – who are generally seeking more affordable bargains – so you can find some good prices. There are six aisles (plus alcoves) containing variety of antiques and collectibles, with more of the latter. The variety in the booths and in between them is a welcome relief to those who hit the flea market next door first, where you grow weary of passing booth after booth touting the same stuff – especially in the kiosks. Sales people open up cases for you here and bring your items to the front where you pay for everything at once. Fine, but you sometimes have to stand here waiting for a sales clerk when you'd rather be shopping.

SHOP NEARBY: Yes, of course the SAMPLE ROAD FLEA MARKET is "nearby." This is inside it.

SINCERELY YOURS

www.sincerelyyoursconsignment.com
11324 S. Federal Hwy. / Pompano Beach 33062 / (954) 755-7001
OPEN: Wed.-Sat. 11-5

Here they sell designer clothing AND home décor, furnishings and original art – usually places are home décor or clothes places mainly. And, oh yes, there's coffee to make you feel at home while you're thinking of how to spruce up your home. (Or your body, if it's clothes you're here for.)

Owners Cindy & Lisa will even help you decide if something's right for you – and they do things right themselves. For example, they have frequent events, such as "Ladies Night" (with various speakers) on the last Friday of the month from 6 to 9. (RSVP first.)

THE SUGAR CHEST ANTIQUE MALL

www.thesugarchestantiquemall.com / Facebook: sugarchest
960 N. Federal Hwy. / Pompano Beach 33062 / (954) 942-8601
OPEN: Mon.-Sat. 10-6; Sun. 12-6

This place is unbelievable! With 200 booths and 30,000 square feet, the showroom just keeps going and going and going. You can find something for $5 (not much) or $5,000 (not much) but most things here cost far far less. It's all well priced and the variety is amazing. There's also plenty of jewelry here, (including real jewelry in display cases up front), and paintings, as well as some furniture and home décor. You'll see unique and can't live-without furniture, clothing, paintings, jewelry, depression glass, silver, gold, dolls & much, much more!

The Sugar Chest has everything: modern, traditional, old, very old... which you can start to feel when you walk through this gargantuan space. But instead of saying to yourself: "When will this end.?" you say "I can't wait to see more" as you pass booth upon booth of diverse dealers offering so much you would never see elsewhere.

NOTE: They also do lamp refurbishing, repair and rewiring.

THE BEST VINTAGE SHOP IN DADE COUNTY

Some told me it was a vintage shop. Or a super high-end consignment shop for women's clothes. A gallery. A place where lots of movie wardrobe people come to dress their stars. It turns out to all be true. And more. This place is an adventure and a destination in itself!

"There are deals here and we're here to help you find them," said a saleswoman at C. MADELEINE'S, a world-famous and extraordinary vintage shop at 13702 Biscayne Blvd., in North Miami Beach, less than 15 minutes from Broward County.

Want a $100,000 evening gown from their couture gown department (one of three evening gown sections)? It's here. Want a $28 pair of earrings? Or a $45 leather clutch bag? You'll find them too. You'll even find sales: once a year they have a huge vintage yard sale. Sign up in their guest book or check their Facebook page.

More Stores

SHOPPING DISTRICTS

ABACOA TOWN CENTER 1155 Main St, Suite 109 / Jupiter 33458 / (561) 627-2799

Abacoa Town Center is a pedestrian-friendly, old fashioned main street offering restaurants, offices and specialty stores that mix easily with the University campus and Roger Dean Stadium.

ATLANTIC AVENUE DISTRICT Atlantic Ave. / Delray Beach 33483 / (561) 279-1380

Traditional downtown shopping, complete with quaint brick sidewalks and gaslight-style street lamps. Featured are gourmet restaurants, cozy bistros and outdoor cafes in addition to boutiques, gift, antique and jewelry shops, and art galleries.

CITYPLACE 700 S. Rosemary Ave. / West Palm Beach 33401 / (561) 366-1000

Reminiscent of an Italian town center, CityPlace is an exciting destination with shops, restaurants, cultural arts theater, and a 20-screen movie theater with IMAX. New restaurants are coming in this year.

CLEMATIS STREET DISTRICT Downtown West Palm Beach / West Palm Beach 33401 / (561) 833-8873

Many shops, galleries, restaurants and clubs located near the Intracoastal Waterway

MIZNER PARK 433 Plaza Real, Ste. 355 / Boca Raton 33432 / (561) 362-0606

Shop and dine at a resort-like atmosphere, and then unwind at the art museum, cinema or outdoor amphitheater.

PGA COMMONS 5520 PGA Blvd. / Palm Beach Gardens 33418 / (561) 630-8630

Delectable restaurants, bistros and cafes with spectacular indoor and outdoor seating. Not to mention all those shops, galleries and a spa. It's between I-95 and the Florida Turnpike.

Goodwill Shops in Southeast Florida

GOODWILL BOCA BOUTIQUE 1662 N. Federal Hwy. / (561) 362-8662

GOODWILL BOCA RATON (LOGGER'S RUN) 11427 W. Palmetto Park Rd. / (561) 488-7760

GOODWILL BOYNTON BEACH 9764-2 S. Military Trail / (561) 740-4407

GOODWILL CORAL SPRINGS 10369 Royal Palm Blvd. / (954) 755-5880

GOODWILL DEERFIELD SUPERSTORE 289 S. Federal Hwy. / (954) 571-2093

GOODWILL DELRAY VINTAGE SHOP 1640 N. Federal Hwy. / (561) 278-3205

GOODWILL FORT LAUDERDALE 9160 W. State Rd., 84 / (954) 472-2367

GOODWILL GREENACRES 6601 Forest Hill Blvd. / (561) 964-5841

GOODWILL HIALEAH 1800 W. 68th St., #106 / (305) 556-4777

GOODWILL – JUPITER SUPER STORE 1280 W. Indiantown Rd. / (561) 748-6614

GOODWILL LAKE PARK 905 US Hwy.1 / (561) 881-4449

GOODWILL (LAKE WORTH) 4519 Lake Worth Rd. / (561) 967-5525

GOODWILL MIAMI 2121 NW 21st St. / (305) 325-9114

GOODWILL MIAMI 6842 SW 40th St. / (305) 661-4222

GOODWILL PALM BEACH (EMBASSY BOUTIQUE) 210 Sunset Ave. / (561) 315-6629

GOODWILL – PALM BEACH GARDENS BOUTIQUE 4224 Northlake Blvd. / (561) 622-2910

GOODWILL RIVIERA BEACH 3500 Broadway / (561) 842-9112

GOODWILL ROYAL PALM BEACH 9920 Belvedere Rd. / (561) 784-2830

GOODWILL SUNRISE 2029 N. University Dr. / (954) 748-5887

GOODWILL WELLINGTON BOUTIQUE 13873 Wellington Trace / (561) 784-9596

GOODWILL WEST PALM BEACH 1837 N. Military Trail / (561) 478-8824

GOODWILL WEST PALM BEACH (DIXIE HWY.,) 3622 S. Dixie Hwy. / (561) 315-6629

GOODWILL – WEST PALM BEACH CLEARANCE CENTER 1897 Old Okeechobee Rd. / (561) 833-1693

SALVATION ARMY FAMILY & SUPERSTORES IN SOUTHEAST FLORIDA

SALVATION ARMY FORT LAUDERDALE 1791 W. Broward Blvd. / (954) 467-5816

SALVATION ARMY HIALEAH 90 W. 23rd St. / (305) 573-4200

SALVATION ARMY LAKE WORTH 4001 Kirk Rd. / (561) 642-1927

SALVATION ARMY MARGATE 320 N. State Rd., 7 / (954) 979-6999

SALVATION ARMY MIAMI 9790 SW 40th St. / (305) 554-9669

SALVATION ARMY PEMBROKE PINES 888 N. University Dr./ (954) 433-2160

SALVATION ARMY POMPANO BEACH 451 E. Copans Rd. / (954) 782-3925

SALVATION ARMY WEST PALM BEACH 655 N. Military Trail / (561) 683-3513 & (561) 734-2132

SHOULD YOU BUY AT AN OUTLET MALL?

Many outlet shops carry "overstocks," which could be items that they made too much of or that didn't sell – which are probably one or two years old. Unfortunately, more and more outlet malls are selling merchandise made specifically for outlets which isn't the same quality as what you'll find in their retail stores.

Dailyfinance.com reported that "a whopping 85% of the merchandise is made specifically for these shops –and they're often not of the same quality in fabric, stitching, lining and buttons.

(If you do go to an outlet, they said that new merchandise comes in Tuesday and Thursday.)

If you want top quality, and the same garment or accessory that's sold in retail stores, you might do better at a consignment shop that only sells 1-2 year old clothes.

About the Author

"The Happy Shopper," **Paulette Cooper Noble**, lives in Palm Beach with her husband, Paul Noble, and her two Imperial Toy Shih tzus, Polo (as in PoloPublishing), and Peek-a-Boo.

She has written 21 books (and over 1,000 articles) on a variety of subjects: *Bargain Shopping in Palm Beach County, Bargain shopping in Fort Lauderdale, Broward & South Palm Beach, Palm Beach Pets & The People Who Love Them, The Scandal of Scientology, 277 Secrets your Dog Wants You To Know, 277 Secrets Your Cat Wants You To Know, The 100 Top Psychics & Astrologers in America,* and *The Medical Detectives.*

She is the winner of seven writing awards, and pens a regular pet column in the *Palm Beach Daily News.*

Her bargain shopping credentials are: after college she once worked at Bloomingdale's for three hours so she could get the 20% employee discount. See. www.paulettecooper.com & www.shoppinginflorida.net.

About the Researchers

Lisa Peterfreund, who assisted in the Broward County and Dade County sections (plus others), is a graduate of Yale University with her masters in environmental science. She enjoys the benefits of "recycling" through exploring consignment and thrift shops for treasures. After a brief stint at Nordstrom's furthering her customer relations skills while enjoying discounts on merchant sales, she parlayed her expertise as a trustee of her small family foundation, and now serves as philanthropic consultant for foundations and nonprofits.

Susan Coleman, who earlier assisted with the North Palm Beach section of this book. has been in the fashion business since she left college. She worked for Neiman Marcus, and ran her own personal shopping business named "Shopping Unlimited." She saved her clients money by "bargain shopping" for them at establishments such as Marshall's, T.J. Maxx, etc.

About the Editor

Paul Noble is a former television programming executive for Lifetime Television, Metromedia and Fox. In Palm Beach, he is on TV and film boards, and he would shop more frequently, but his wife has taken up all the closet space. He has co-written four books with her, and takes photos for her *Palm Beach Daily News* pet column ("Palm Beach People,") and travel writing. He is the winner of five Emmys for producing and writing. See www.paulrnoble.com.

Interview With Paulette Cooper Noble, The Happy Shopper

When did you begin going to South Florida consignment and vintage shops?
I lived in New York but my parents had a condo in Palm Beach and I visited them over the holidays. I found that the shops down here were better than the ones up north, so I raced to them whenever I came here.

When did you discover how good the resale shops down here are? My mother did volunteer work at a charity shop in Palm Beach. One day Ivana Trump's secretary donated five evening gowns worth $5,000 each – which they priced at $100 apiece. Mom called me to come over immediately, and after that, she began to call me to come over when something like a Hermes bag came in. I was hooked.

What made you write about these places? When I moved down here I had already written 15 books. I decided not to write any more because they were too much work. I kept waiting for someone else to write a guide book to all these wonderful shops so I could read it but no one did. So I figured it wouldn't be too much work (WRONG) because I was going to these places and knew them anyway.

Can't people get information about these shops free from the internet?
That's what I thought at first. But when I tried to locate shops online, I found that three-quarters of the listings were incorrect or incomplete. And it was frustrating to drive all the way to a shop that sounded great and find out that they had closed two years before.

In addition, it's hard to tell from the Internet whether there are good resale shops near the one they're going to, and they don't give special shopping tour suggestions as I do.

What extra information do you give people in this book that they can't easily find elsewhere? When the shops have special sales and where the sale merchandise is in the store, directions on how to get to some if it's complicated , shopping tour suggestions so people can go to a few great places in one area, and most important, what similar places are nearby. I always hated learning that I had missed a great consignment shop a few doors down while I was shopping at another one.

When did you begin consignment shopping? When I left college I lived at 80th Street between 5th & Madison Avenue in New York. ENCORE, the first real consignment shop, was at 84th & Madison. So I began going there– so frequently, that one of my friends commented that she didn't think I'd ever marry because there were no wedding dresses at Encore.

Why do you like bargain shopping? You've heard the expression: the pursuit of happiness? For many of us, it's the happiness of pursuit.

— Paulette Cooper Noble

Notes

CPSIA information can be obtained at www.ICGtesting.com
Printed in the USA
LVOW04s0239091015

457581LV00002B/7/P